I0704832

The Path To Peace:

Overcoming Mental Health Challenges

Where To Download The EBook Version

Thank you for reading 21 Steps to Mental Wellness: Overcoming Common Challenges. I hope this book helped you understand and conquer your mental health issues.

If you enjoyed this book and want a digital copy for future reference or to share with friends and family, you can purchase the eBook edition on Amazon Kindle.

Here's how to download the eBook:

1. Visit Amazon Kindle. Go to amazon.com and look for " Overcoming mental health Challenges" by Oyerogba Oyetayo Olamide.

2. Select the eBook version: Once you've discovered the book, choose the Kindle edition to read it in eBook format.

3. Purchase and Download: To get the eBook, click the "Buy now with 1-Click" option. Once purchased, the eBook will be available for download to your Kindle or any device that supports the Kindle app.

4. Enjoy Reading: You may now read the eBook on your Kindle, smartphone, tablet, or computer, making it easy to access whenever you need it.

For additional information and updates, please reach me via email oyetayoolamideblog@gmail.com or sign up for my newsletter. You can also visit my amazon page to see other books by me https://rb.gy/6bw1jf

Thank you for your support, and best wishes on your path to mental wellness. Oyerogba Oyetayo Olamide

The Path To Peace:

Overcoming Mental Health Challenges

Paperback ISBN: 9798340846389

EBook ISBN: [Insert ISBN]

First Edition in 2024

Oyerogba Oyetayo Olamide

Email address: Oyetayoolamideblog@gmail.com

[

All Rights Reserved Statement:

21 Steps to Mental Wellness: Overcoming Common Challenges

Copyright © 2024 by Oyerogba Oyetayo Olamide

All rights reserved. No part of this book may be reproduced, distributed, or transmitted in any form or by any means, including photocopying, recording, or other electronic or mechanical methods, without the prior written permission of the publisher. This book may not be lent, resold, hired out, or otherwise disposed of by way of trade in any form of binding or cover other than that in which it is published without the prior written consent of the publisher.

For permission requests, write to the publisher, addressed "Attention: Permissions Coordinator," at the address below:

Email: oyetayoolamideblog@gmail.com

Disclaimer:

This book is intended for informational and educational purposes only and should not be used as a substitute for professional medical or psychological advice. If you or someone you know is struggling with mental health issues, it is essential to seek help from a licensed healthcare professional. The author is not a licensed therapist or medical professional, and the information provided in this book should not be interpreted as medical or psychological guidance.

The author and publisher shall not be held liable for any damages, negative effects, or consequences arising from the use or misuse of the information contained in this book. Always consult a qualified professional before making any decisions or taking any actions related to mental health or well-being.

This book is a work of fiction. Names, characters, places, and incidents are the product of the author's imagination or are used fictitiously. Any resemblance to actual persons, living or dead, events, or locales is purely coincidental.

DEDICATION

To everyone who has ever faced a mental health challenge and felt alone in the struggle—this book is for you.

To those who have fought, fallen, and risen again—your resilience inspires the world.

And to my family and friends, whose unwavering support has carried me through my own journey—I am forever grateful.

May this book serve as a reminder that you are never truly alone and that healing is always possible.

CONTENTS

"Mental health...is not a destination, but a process. It's about how you drive, not where you're going."

— Noam Shpancer

"There is hope, even when your brain tells you there isn't."

— John Green

"Healing doesn't mean the damage never existed. It means the damage no longer controls our lives."

— Akshay Dubey

INTRODUCTION:

The Greatest Way to Understand Mental health and its Challenges

Welcome to the *21 Steps to Mental Wellness: Overcoming Common Challenges*. I am happy you have taken up this book. Maybe you're here because you've been dealing with your mental health or want to know more about it. Whatever the reason, I'd like to tell you that this book is for you.

What is mental health?

Let us define mental wellness. Mental health refers to our emotional, psychological, and social well-being. It has an impact on how we think, feel, and behave in everyday situations. It also determines how we deal with stress, communicate with people, and make decisions. Mental health is equally important as physical health; however, it is commonly overlooked or misunderstood.

We all have physical and mental health. It's good on occasion, but not always. And that is fine. What is important is that we realize when we aren't feeling our best and understand that requesting help and support is perfectly normal.

Why is Mental Health Important?

Mental health is a crucial part of our overall health. It affects everything we do, from our daily routines to our long-term goals. When our mental health is good, we feel more prepared to tackle life's challenges. We may spend time with our loved ones, concentrate on our careers, and follow our passions. However, as our mental health deteriorates, everything becomes much more difficult.

Imagine you're lugging a heavy backpack. When you're in good mental health, your backpack contains lightweight, controlled substances. However, while dealing with mental health concerns, it may feel as if your backpack is full of stones, weighing you down with every step.

Common Mental Health Challenges.

What are these "mental health challenges" that we hear about? Mental health diseases come in a variety of types. Anxiety, sadness, and stress are among the most prevalent, along with obsessive-compulsive disorder (OCD) and bipolar disorder. Each of these worries has a unique influence on people, but they all have one thing: they can make daily living feel overwhelming.

Anxiety

Anxiety is one of the most common mental health concerns. It's more than just being nervous before a big test or presentation. For others, anxiety is a constant companion, making even ordinary tasks appear intimidating. It may cause physical symptoms such as heartbeat, sweat, and difficulty breathing. It can also disrupt attention and sleep.

Depression

Depression isn't only about being sad or having a bad day. It is distinguished by a persistent sensation of despair, hopelessness, or a loss of interest in formerly enjoyable activities. Depression can make it difficult to get out of bed in the morning, maintain motivation, or even satisfy basic needs. It is a dangerous condition, but it is treatable.

Stress

Stress is something that everyone experiences from time to time. It is the body's response to any demand or challenge. A little stress can be motivating, but too much stress, especially if it is chronic, can be harmful to our mental and physical health. It can result in worry, depression, and physical health problems like heart disease.

Why do we suffer with our mental health?

Someone may struggle with their mental health for a variety of reasons. It can be the outcome of a specific incident, such as losing a loved one, going through a breakup, or facing a significant life change. Long-term stress, such as financial challenges, job pressure, or family problems, may also be to blame.

Mental health issues can also be linked to biology; certain people are predisposed to anxiety or depression owing to heredity or brain chemistry. Let us not underestimate the power of our surroundings and experiences, such as trauma or abuse, which can leave lasting emotional scars.

Breaking the stigma.

One of the most important challenges is the stigma associated with mental health. For far too long, mental illnesses have been stigmatized and ignored. But here's the truth: it's not humiliating to struggle with your mental health. Similarly, it is not shameful to have a broken leg or a persistent sickness.

The first step in reducing the stigma connected with mental health is to openly discuss the topic. It tells us that we are not alone and that we can ask for help. This book provides a safe space for us to discuss such topics, learn more about mental health, and devise techniques to care for ourselves and one another.

Why this book?

You may be wondering what makes this book different from others on mental health. The answer is straightforward: this book is about actual people and their tales. It is about sharing experiences that we can all relate to, whether we have been there ourselves or know someone who has.

Each chapter of this book will introduce you to a new narrative, which may sound quite similar to your own or someone you know. Each story contains useful suggestions and ideas for improving your own mental health or helping others.

A Journey to Wellness

Mental wellness is not a destination, but rather a process. Some days will be enjoyable; others will be miserable. But it's fine. What matters is that we continue to progress, taking small steps toward wellness. Also, keep in mind that it is acceptable to seek help when needed. We're all in this together.

As you read this book, I hope you find comfort, understanding, and maybe even inspiration. I hope you understand that no matter what you are going through, you are not alone. Most importantly, I hope you find the strength to take the next step forward in your mental health, whatever it may be.

So let us start this trip together. Let us learn, grow, and help one other along the road. Everyone is entitled to live their best, healthiest lives.

Welcome to the first step in better understanding and managing your mental health. Let's dive in.

THE POWER OF SHARING OUR STORIES

Sharing our story is one of the most powerful tools we have for achieving mental well-being. When we open up about our challenges, we not only lessen our own burden but also help others understand they are not alone. The chapters in this book are filled with experiences from people who have faced a variety of mental health challenges—stories that may be similar to your own or introduce you to perspectives you had not previously considered.

These are not only stories of grief, but also of fortitude, healing, and optimism. They show that no matter how bleak things appear, there is always a path forward. Reading about these experiences may give you the motivation you need to take the next step in your own journey. And perhaps, in time, you will be encouraged to share your own story with others, so contributing to the reduction of stigma and isolation associated with mental health issues.

Understanding the breadth of mental health concerns.

Mental health diseases are quite prevalent. In fact, it is estimated that one in every four people may experience a mental health issue at some point in their lives. Despite their prevalence, these illnesses are often misunderstood or ignored. This is due to the stigma I previously mentioned, as well as the fact that mental health can be difficult to detect. Unlike physical ailments, mental health issues do not often result in evident symptoms. They are easily hidden, even from ourselves.

This is why understanding mental health is essential. By educating ourselves and others on mental health issues, how they affect us, and how they may be treated, we can begin to tear down the barriers that keep people from seeking help. Whether it's detecting anxiety signs in a friend, understanding the effects of depression, or learning how to deal with stress in our own lives, information is a great tool for improving mental health for everyone.

What You'll Discover in This Book

Each of the 21 chapters in this book focuses on a different aspect of mental health, from understanding anxiety and depression to stress management and resilience development. Each chapter consists of the following:

A personal narrative: Each chapter begins with a true-life story from someone who has experienced the mental health issue under review. These stories are intended to be approachable and honest, providing insight into people's lived experiences with mental health concerns.

* Insights and Information: Following the story, each chapter delves deeper into the particulars of the mental health condition, explaining what it is, how it manifests, and why it occurs. This section is designed to help you understand the problem from a psychological and emotional standpoint.

* Practical tactics: Each chapter concludes with practical guidance and strategies for managing and overcoming mental health issues. These ideas are based on both expert guidance and the lived experiences of those who

have been there, providing you with a diverse set of tools to pick from.

A Path Forward

The goal of this book is to not only offer facts but also to recommend a path forward. Mental health difficulties can seem overwhelming, but it is critical to remember that there is always hope. With the right support, resources, and perspective, you can get through even the most difficult moments.

Take your time reading this book and focus on each chapter. Reflect on the stories, think about how the information applies to your own life, and try out the strategies that appeal to you. Remember that this is a journey, and it's okay to go at your own pace.

If you are reading this book because you are struggling with your mental health, please know that you are not alone. Help is available, and recovery is possible. Thank you for taking the time to learn about your loved one's concerns. Your assistance can make all the difference.

Moving Forward Together

To conclude, I want to thank you for taking the first step on this journey by purchasing this book. Mental health is a challenging and deeply personal issue that impacts all of us. We may have a significant influence by learning more about it, sharing our stories, and supporting one another—not just in our own lives, but also in the lives of those around us.

Let us move forward together, with respect, understanding, and a commitment to improving our mental health. There are 23 steps ahead of us, each with new ideas, tools, and optimism. I'm honored to be on this adventure with you.

Let's begin.

Part 1: Understanding Mental Health and Embracing Awareness

1.

Recognizing Anxiety

"Anxiety may feel like an unwelcome companion, but by facing it head-on, we discover the strength to reclaim our peace and transform fear into resilience."

Relatable Story: Emily's Overwhelming Anxiety

Emily sat in the back row of her crowded lecture hall, her hands gripping her pen so tightly that her knuckles became white. The professor's voice was a distant buzz in her ears, and she could only hear the fast pounding of her own heartbeat. Her chest felt heavy as if a weight was pressing down on her, making breathing difficult. It happened again: panic attack.

Emily had been experiencing anxiety on a regular basis since commencing university. She had always been an excellent student in high school, but college was different. The pressure to succeed, the never-ending stream of assignments, and the fear of disappointing her family were affecting her mental health. Every night, she'd lie awake in bed, her mind racing with scenarios for what could go wrong.

"What happens if I fail my exams? What if I am not cut out for this? "What if everyone realizes I'm an imposter?" These thoughts would play over and over in her mind until she felt like she was drowning in them. Anxiety was like a steady background noise, humming around.

Social circumstances were not any easier. Emily found herself avoiding gatherings and celebrations, even when she wanted to attend. The thought of being among people, having to make conversation, and pretending to be fine seemed like an impossible feat. She was afraid of saying the wrong thing or seeming silly, so she spent much of her time alone in her dorm room.

Emily decided to attend a study group at the library one evening, expecting that being with others would help her focus. When she walked in and saw her pals conversing and laughing, a wave of fear washed over her. Her palms began to sweat, her heartbeat, and her vision blurred. She quickly apologized and hurried to the nearest lavatory, locking herself in a stall and trying to catch her breath.

Emily felt completely alone as she sat on the icy tile floor. "Why can't I just be normal?" she asked herself. "Why is this happening to me?" She knew she couldn't keep living this way, but she wasn't sure where to start.

Understanding Anxiety: The First Step to Overcoming It

If Emily's story seems familiar, you're not alone. Anxiety is one of the most common mental health conditions, affecting millions around the world. It comes in many different forms, including generalized anxiety disorder (GAD), social anxiety, panic disorders, and phobias. Recognizing anxiety is the first step towards overcoming it.

Anxiety might feel like a mental storm, filled with uncontrollable thoughts and fears. It usually begins with a trigger—a stressful situation, an upsetting thought, or even an abrupt shift. It can then quickly escalate, causing harm to both your mental and physical health. Anxiety symptoms include rapid heartbeat, shortness of breath, sweating, and dizziness.

Anxiety, however, is more than just panic attacks or nervousness; it is also the ongoing, underlying worry that can cloud your judgment and interfere with your daily life.

Some people, including Emily, are terrified of failing or falling short of their aspirations. Others may be apprehensive about their social standing or the future. Whatever the cause, the consequences can be severe, making it difficult to focus, enjoy life, or even get out of bed in the morning.

Strategies for Overcoming Anxiety

The good news is that anxiety can be managed, and there are effective methods for recovering control. Here are some practical techniques to manage anxiety:

1. Deep Breathing Exercises:

Deep breathing is one of the most simple and efficient methods for anxiety management. When you are anxious, your body goes into "fight or flight" mode, causing you to breathe shallowly and rapidly. Deep breathing relaxes your nervous system and reduces the physical symptoms of anxiety.

- Attempt this: Sit down and close your eyes. Take a slow, deep breath through your nose, filling your lungs completely. Hold your breath for four counts before exhaling slowly through your mouth. Repeat this approach five to ten times, concentrating on your breath and relaxing your body with each exhale.

2. Cognitive-Behavioral Techniques (CBT):

Cognitive-behavioral therapy (CBT) is an effective technique for dealing with anxiety. It requires recognizing and confronting the negative thoughts that generate concern. You may change your emotions by changing your way of thinking.

- Try this: When you begin to feel anxious, write down what is going through your mind. Do you imagine the worst-case scenario? Are you overestimating the likelihood of anything bad happening? Once you've jotted down your ideas, challenge them. Ask yourself: "Is this thought based on facts or assumptions?" "What evidence do I have that this will happen?" "Is there another way to look at this situation?"

3. Seeking Professional Help:

Anxiety can be overpowering at times, and self-help strategies alone may not be sufficient. In these cases, seeking professional help from a therapist or counselor can have a major influence. Therapy provides a safe setting in which to express your emotions, learn new coping strategies, and address underlying issues that may be causing your anxiety.

- Try this: If your anxiety is interfering with your quality of life, don't hesitate to seek treatment. Many colleges and towns offer free or low-cost counseling services. Remember that asking for help shows strength, not weakness.

4. Mindfulness and Grounding Techniques:

Mindfulness entails keeping present in the moment while being aware of your thoughts and emotions without passing judgment. Grounding methods may help you stay present and prevent your thoughts from wandering into anxiety.

- Try this: Concentrate your attention on your surroundings. Describe what you see, hear, smell, taste, and feel, whether aloud or to yourself. For example: "I see a blue chair," "I hear birds chirping," and "I feel the texture of my shirt." This technique might help you focus on the present moment and reduce worry.

5. Creating a Routine:

Setting up a daily routine can provide structure and predictability, which can help to reduce anxiety. Plan time for self-care, hobbies, and relaxation in your everyday routine.

Try this: Make a daily schedule that includes time for work or study, meals, exercise, social activities, and rest. Routines may help you feel more in control and less overwhelmed by uncertainty.

Moving Forward: You're Not Alone

Emily's journey did not finish at the library's washroom. She sought help from a university counselor, who explained her anxieties and gave her coping methods. With time and practice, she learned to manage her anxiety and began to feel more like herself. She still feels anxious, but she knows what to do and where to get help.

Remember that anxiety is not a sign of weakness or something to be embarrassed about. It is a common human emotion that may be controlled with the right tools and support. If you are feeling anxious, know that you are not alone and that help is available. Take things one step at a time and be kind to yourself. Healing is a continual process, and any progress, no matter how small, is a step in the right direction.

As you read through this book, you will come across more stories like Emily's, as well as tools and insights to help you navigate the complexities of mental health. Let's take this journey together, one chapter at a time.

Finding Support: Building a Network

Having a support system is vital while dealing with anxiety. Emily found comfort in her friends and family after she began to open up about her problems. She was originally concerned that people would misunderstand or condemn her. However, when she finally confided in her roommate, she was surprised by the reaction.

"I had no idea you were going through this," Emily's roommate said softly, reaching out to hold her hand. "But I am here for you. We will figure out whatever you need together."

Emily's life has transformed as a result of that talk. She realized that others truly cared about her and wanted to help. She began conversing with her parents, sharing her feelings. They, too, offered their support and encouragement, reminding her that she was not alone and that they were proud of her for seeking help.

- Try this: Contact a trusted friend, family member, or mentor. Tell them about your experiences. Just talking about what you're going through can help relieve stress. You might be amazed at how many people have faced similar challenges and are prepared to assist.

Understanding Triggers: Know What Sets Off Your Anxiety

Emily's life has transformed as a result of their chat. She realized that others truly cared about her and wanted to help. She began talking to her parents about her feelings. They, too, conveyed their support and encouragement, reminding her that she was not alone and that they were proud of her for seeking help.

- Try this: Please talk to a trustworthy friend, family member, or mentor. Tell them about your experiences. Simply talking about what you're going through can help reduce stress. You might be amazed at how many people have faced similar challenges and are eager to assist.

Try this: Start a journal to keep track of your anxiety episodes. Write down what you were doing, where you were, who you were with, and what you were thinking when your anxiety started. Over time, you'll begin to notice patterns and recognize your triggers. Understanding what causes your anxiety is a significant step toward treatment.

Embracing Self-Care: It's Not Just About Bubble Baths

Self-care entails more than just pampering oneself; it also includes taking care of your mental, emotional, and physical health. Emily included self-care in her daily routine. She learned to listen to her body and mind, enabling herself to rest and relax as needed.

She began going for daily walks in the park, seeking peace in nature and allowing herself to relax. She also began doing yoga, which made her feel more balanced and peaceful. Emily learned that prioritizing her well-being helped her manage her anxiety.

Try this: Make a list of self-care activities that you enjoy and that leave you feeling refreshed and energized. This could be reading a book, taking a bath, meditating, or going for a walk. Plan these events into your daily schedule as you would any other important appointment. Taking time for oneself is not selfish; it is necessary for your overall well-being.

The Role of Diet and Exercise in Managing Anxiety

Emily's recovery also includes careful attention to her diet and exercise regimen. She found that her eating habits and movement patterns had a big impact on her anxiety levels. On days when she ate well and exercised, she felt more energized and less anxious.

She began including more fruits and vegetables, healthful grains, and lean proteins into her diet while avoiding excessive sugar and caffeine, which she discovered might exacerbate her anxiety. Exercise became a part of her everyday regimen, whether it was a 15-minute jog or a quick yoga class.

Try this: Pay attention to how various foods and activities affect your mood. Maintain a weekly diet and activity record, noting how you feel after each meal and workout. You may discover that particular foods or exercises help you feel less anxious. Add more of these to your routine and see how they influence your mental health.

Moving Forward with Confidence

Emily's road was not straightforward, and it did not happen overnight. Some days, she felt as if she were taking two steps forward and one back. However, with time, determination, and assistance, she was able to overcome her fears. She understood that asking for help was acceptable and that her mental health was a priority.

She began attending a support group for students suffering from anxiety, where she met others who had experienced similar experiences. Sharing her story and hearing other people's made her feel less alone and more empowered. She also persisted in her treatment sessions, eventually establishing a set of anxiety-management techniques.

- Consider joining a support group or finding an online community where you may connect with others going through similar experiences. Sharing your experiences and hearing from others can foster a sense of community and support, which is extremely valuable.

As you continue reading, remember that anxiety alleviation is a journey. It's about determining what works best for you, whether that's deep breathing, mindfulness, therapy, or emotional support from loved ones. Be patient with yourself, and celebrate small achievements. Your worry does not define you; you can live a fulfilling, joyful life.

This chapter is only the beginning. As we progress, you'll discover new tales, strategies, and insights to help you navigate the complex world of mental health. Remember that you are not alone, and together we can face the obstacles that lie ahead. Continue turning the pages, and let us take this journey together, one step at a time.

2.

Battling Depression

"Depression is not the end of your story—it's a chapter. And with each small step forward, you write a new page filled with hope, healing, and possibility."

Relatable Story: David's Struggle with Depression

David gazed blankly at the ceiling, his body heavy and immovable. The alarm clock had been ringing for a while, but he couldn't get the strength to turn it off. It was Monday morning, and the sun was shining through the blinds, signaling the start of the new day. However, David saw it as just another challenge to overcome. Getting out of bed, showering, and addressing the world seemed impossible.

David, once vibrant and active, was now a shadow of himself. He used to enjoy playing soccer with his children on weekends, cooking lavish dinners for his family, and gathering with friends for a game of poker. But now, even the things he once enjoyed appeared pointless. His world had lost its color, and everything looked dull and drab.

David's wife, Lisa, noticed the changes in him. He'd become withdrawn, spending most of his time in bed or on the sofa. He rarely laughed or smiled anymore, and when he did speak, it was usually in short, flat words. His lack of enthusiasm and excitement worried her, but every time she asked if he was all right, he disregarded it, stating he was just tired or stressed.

However, David recognized it was more than that. He was lost in his own mind, plagued by an overwhelming sense of sadness and hopelessness. There were days when he felt like a failure as if he had disappointed everyone. He loathed feeling this way but didn't know how to stop it. The more he tried to push these feelings away, the stronger they seemed to get.

Lisa sat by David on the couch one evening, as he was staring at the TV without really watching it. "David, I'm really worried about you," she replied softly. "You haven't been yourself lately, and I can see you're hurting. Please chat with me. Allow me to help you."

David felt a knot forming in his throat. He wanted to tell her everything, to reveal the darkness that had seized him. But he was terrified. Afraid of being judged and perceived as weak. Instead, he shook his head and muttered, "I am alright. Do not worry about me."

But Lisa wouldn't give up. She placed her hand on his and whispered, "David, you're not alone. Whatever happens, I will be here for you. We can go through this together.

Understanding Depression: The Silent Struggle

David's story is one that many people can relate to. Depression is a silent struggle that is frequently hidden beneath a façade of normalcy. It affects individuals of various ages, genders, and origins. It's more than just being miserable or having a bad day; it's an ongoing sensation of emptiness, pessimism, and alienation from the world around you.

Depression can manifest in a variety of ways, including a lack of energy, difficulty concentrating, changes in eating or sleeping habits, and a loss of interest in formerly enjoyable activities. It can make even the most simple activities appear unattainable. Others, such as David, may experience a numbness that pervades all aspects of their lives, and others may have an intense melancholy that is difficult to overcome.

One of the most difficult aspects of depression is the tendency to isolate. It can leave you feeling alone in your pain as if no one else understands what you're going through. This isolation can create a vicious cycle in which the more alienated you feel, the more difficult it is to seek assistance.

Strategies for Overcoming Depression

While depression might feel overwhelming and unpleasant, it is important to remember that it is manageable and treatable. There are a variety of strategies and activities you can use to help remove the fog of depression and begin the path to recovery.

1. Acknowledging the Problem: The First Step to Healing

Recognizing that you are suffering from depression is the first and most crucial step toward recovery. For David, this insight occurred when he finally admitted to himself and Lisa that he was not only tired or stressed, but also depressed.

Try this: Take a moment to check in with yourself. How have you been feeling lately? Have you seen any shifts in your mood, energy level, or interest in specific activities? If you believe you are suffering from depression, you must acknowledge and address the issue. Depression is not a sign of weakness, and admitting it is a brave and necessary step.

2. Establishing a Routine: Bringing Structure to Your Day

One of the symptoms of depression is a lack of motivation, which can make it difficult to get out of bed and finish daily tasks. Routines can provide structure and a sense of purpose, making it easier to manage your time.

- **Try this:** Create a simple daily schedule that includes essential activities such as getting up, eating, and sleeping at the same time every day. Include small, manageable tasks like taking a shower, going on a walk, or finishing a project. Creating a schedule can help to reestablish a sense of normalcy and reduce the overwhelming symptoms of depression.

3. Exercise: Moving Your Body to Improve Your Mind

Exercise may be the last thing you want to do when you're depressed, yet it's one of the most effective natural ways to boost your mood. Physical activity induces the release of endorphins, which are brain chemicals that improve mood and alleviate pain.

Try this: Begin small. You don't need to run a marathon or spend hours in the gym. Even a simple walk around the block or light stretching will help. Choose an activity that you enjoy and incorporate it into your everyday routine. Over time, you may discover that regular exercise makes you feel more energized and less down.

4. Connecting with Loved Ones: Breaking the Isolation

Depression often drives people to withdraw from others, but staying in touch with loved ones is essential. A support system can provide comfort, understanding, and a sense of community.

Try this: Reach out to a friend or family member, even if it is just to talk or meet for coffee. If you aren't ready to talk about your depression, simply being around people who care about you can be enough. If you feel safe, consider sharing your feelings with someone you trust. They may be able to help or direct you to the resources you need.

5. Seeking Professional Help: Therapy and Medication

For many people, obtaining professional help is an important part of addressing depression. Therapists, counselors, and psychiatrists are trained to help you understand your feelings, develop coping strategies, and address any underlying issues causing your melancholy.

- **Try This:** If you're struggling with depression, speak with a mental health professional. Therapy can provide a safe place in which to explore your thoughts and feelings, whilst medication can help control the chemicals in your brain that influence mood. Remember that asking for help shows strength, not weakness.

David's Journey: A Glimmer of Hope

David's recuperation was not a straight line, and it did not happen immediately. After talking with Lisa, he made an appointment with his doctor, who referred him to a therapist. David was initially hesitant, wondering if talking about his feelings would help. But, with time, he came to see the benefits.

During treatment, David learned to identify the negative thought patterns that were creating his sadness. He realized he was carrying a lot of guilt and shame about his perceived flaws, which were dragging him down. He learned via cognitive-behavioral therapy (CBT) to challenge these beliefs and replace them with more balanced, realistic ones.

He also began taking tiny steps to improve his daily routine. He began getting up at the same time every day, regardless of whether he felt like it, and incorporating exercise into his regimen. He began with a quick walk around the block, then moved to running and even joining a local soccer club.

David had trouble connecting with others, but he tried to spend more time with his family and friends. He noticed that discussing his concerns with Lisa reduced his stress, and spending time with his children reminded him of what was most essential.

Moving Forward: You Are Not Alone

If you're feeling depressed, know that you're not alone. It's okay to feel your emotions and seek help. Depression may make you feel as if you are trapped in a dark tunnel, yet there is an exit. Acknowledging your emotions, creating a routine, exercising, connecting with loved ones, and seeking professional support can all help you see the light at the end of the tunnel.

David's experience shows that recovery is possible and there is hope. It's a unique process for each person, but with time, support, and the right tools, you may overcome sadness and start feeling more like yourself.

Creating a Supportive Environment: Surrounding Yourself with Positivity

One of the most crucial components of managing depression is to foster a happy and supportive environment. David learned that his familial environment had a significant impact on his mental health. As he began to make changes, he concentrated on surrounding himself with things and people who motivated him.

David and Lisa transformed their home into a more calming and inviting environment. They redecorated the living room with bright colors and added personal touches to remind David of happier times. They also set up a tiny alcove with relaxing stuff like comfortable seats, a lovely blanket, and a few novels that David liked. This location became a haven for David to unwind and clear his mind.

Try this: Examine your environment for any elements that may be causing your tension or sadness. Consider making changes to make your environment more pleasant. It might be as simple as adding plants, rearranging furniture for better lighting, or creating a cozy alcove to relax in. A positive setting has a significant influence on your attitude and motivation.

Setting Small, Achievable Goals: Building Momentum

Depression may make even little tasks seem onerous. David's therapist urged him to set small, manageable goals in order to regain momentum and a sense of accomplishment. This strategy helped him overcome the immobility that often accompanied his grief.

David set little goals, such as getting out of bed and showering every day. As his confidence grew, he set new goals for himself, such as making meals or tidying his room. Celebrating these small victories gave him a sense of accomplishment and increased his confidence.

- **Try this**: Set small, manageable goals for yourself each day. These could include changing your bed, going for a little walk, or calling a friend. Break down large tasks into smaller steps and focus on completing one at a time. Recognize and celebrate your accomplishments, no matter how modest they may seem. Every step forward is a success.

Practicing Mindfulness: Staying Present

Mindfulness became an important aspect of David's rehabilitation process. It helped him stay grounded and focused, which lowered the intensity of his negative thoughts. David employed mindfulness techniques to notice his thoughts without judgment and stay in the present moment.

David gained consciousness through meditation and deep breathing techniques. He set aside time every day to sit quietly, concentrate on his breathing, and let go of the racing thoughts that were bothering him. This practice helped him gain a feeling of serenity and perspective, allowing him to better control his emotions.

- **Try This:** Incorporate mindfulness practices into your regular routine. Begin with a few minutes of meditation or deep breathing every day. If you're not sure where to start, consider apps or guided videos. Mindfulness can help you focus on the present moment and reduce the impact of negative thoughts.

Finding Joy in Small Things: Rediscovering Passion

Depression can take away the delight you once had from ordinary tasks. Reconnecting with simple joys and interests was a key part of David's rehabilitation. He began to consider activities that he had once enjoyed but had lost interest in.

David discovered his love of gardening. He started with a few small plants and found that caring for them provided him with a sense of accomplishment and calm. He also resumed former activities, such as reading and playing the guitar, which provided him with a sense of success and pleasure.

- **Attempt This:** Reconnect with formerly pleasurable activities, or try new ones that tickle your interest. Engage in hobbies, creative projects, or leisure activities that provide you pleasure and satisfaction. Even small moments of joy can boost your overall well-being.

Seeking Professional Help: Therapy and Medication

David's path involves getting professional help, which proved to be a critical turning point. His therapist created a safe atmosphere for him to express his emotions and develop coping mechanisms. Medication also helped him deal with his issues.

It's vital to understand that seeking professional help is a proactive and helpful step. Therapists and psychiatrists are trained to assist people with their mental health issues and can provide valuable skills and assistance. David's decision to seek therapy demonstrated his fortitude and desire to improve his quality of life.

- **Try This:** If you're battling with depression, talk to a mental health expert. Therapy and medication can help to relieve depression and enhance overall well-being. Don't be afraid to seek treatment; it's a sign of strength and an important step toward recovery.

Building Resilience: Learning and Growing From Experience

As David continued on his search, he developed resilience. He learned that, while depression was a difficult task, it also provided chances for personal growth and discovery. David discovered more about himself and his needs via therapy, self-care, and family support.

David's resilience was not about completely overcoming depression, but about learning how to navigate its challenges and emerge stronger. He learned new coping skills, new perspectives on life, and a deeper appreciation for the assistance he received.

Try this: Reflect on your personal journey and recognize the strengths and resilience you've developed along the way. Accept the growth and learning that comes from conquering adversity. Building resilience can help you face future problems with more confidence and strength.

David's Path to Hope: A Message of Encouragement

David's experience serves as a reminder that recovery from depression is possible. It requires patience, effort, and support, but it is doable. David was able to reclaim his life and find hope by recognizing his difficulties, seeking treatment, and taking decisive action.

If you are struggling with depression, realize that you are not alone. Your journey may be difficult, but there is help and hope. Take it one step at a time, ask for support, and believe in your ability to overcome this challenge.

As you read this book, keep in mind that each chapter includes strategies and insights to help you navigate the complexities of mental health. Your recovery journey is unique, and each step leads you closer to a happier, more fulfilling future.

3.

Coping With Social Anxiety

"Overcoming social anxiety isn't about becoming the loudest person in the room—it's about finding the courage to connect with others on your own terms, one step at a time."

Sarah stood at the entrance to the crowded party, clutching the strap of her purse so tightly that her knuckles turned white. She had been invited by a coworker and didn't want to look disrespectful by declining, but now that she was there, the all-too-familiar feeling of panic washed over her. Her heart raced, her palms grew clammy, and the cacophony of laughter and chatter was overwhelming. Every fiber of her being pleaded with her to leave and seek sanctuary in her apartment, where she was the only one judging herself.

Sarah had felt this way before. Over time, social gatherings have become a source of terror. She'd stand in the corner of the room, avoiding eye contact and unsure how to begin a conversation or deal with the anxiety that was developing inside her. Every look in her direction brought a harsh judgment to mind. *They believe I'm awkward. They are asking why I am even here. What will happen if I say something stupid?

As the evening went on, Sarah remained glued to the side of the room, pretending to check her phone while people milled around her. She knew she wasn't making the most of the evening, but the thought of trying to join a group conversation filled her with dread, and all she could think about was when it was time to leave.

Sarah's life was dominated by her social anxiety. She avoided speaking out in meetings at work because she was afraid her peers would reject her ideas. In social situations, she felt like an outsider, unable to join in the fun. Her worry was a continual impediment to building meaningful relationships and left her feeling lonely.

However, this narrative is about Sarah's journey to understand and overcome her social anxiety.

Understanding Social Anxiety

Social anxiety refers to more than just shyness or discomfort in social situations. It is the overwhelming fear of being judged, rejected, or humiliated in social or performance contexts. People with social anxiety frequently experience significant worry in daily situations such as attending a party, speaking in public, or even making small talk with a coworker.

Sarah's social anxiety sprang from an intense fear of embarrassment. Every time she entered a social setting, her imagination raced over every possible scenario in which she could be judged or mocked. This fear would worsen, locking her in her thoughts and preventing her from appreciating the present moment.

Symptoms of social anxiety can vary, but common signs include:

- Intense fear or anxiety in social situations

- Avoidance of social events or situations

- Physical symptoms like a racing heart, sweating, trembling, or dizziness

- Negative self-talk and fear of being judged or embarrassed

While many people are uncomfortable in certain settings, social anxiety becomes problematic when it interferes with daily life and relationships. Sarah's anxiety was more than just unpleasant; it was keeping her from leading the life she sought.

Sarah's Approach to Overcoming Social Anxiety.

Sarah realized she couldn't keep living this way after a particularly stressful evening in which she had to leave a friend's wedding early due to nerves. She knew she needed help, but the prospect of talking to someone about her social anxiety was scary. However, after weeks of internal strife, she decided to consult an anxiety problem professional.

The first step in Sarah's journey was identifying the source of her concern. During treatment, she discovered that her social anxiety was fueled by perfectionism and a fear of rejection. She felt forced to present herself as flawless in order to avoid criticism, but this pressure just exacerbated her concerns. Her therapist introduced her to cognitive-behavioral therapy (CBT), a therapeutic approach that helps people challenge and overcome negative thought patterns.

One of Sarah's first exercises was exposure therapy. Her therapist recommended she gradually expose herself to the social situations that caused her anxiety, starting with small, manageable steps. Rather than forcing herself to attend enormous parties, Sarah began with more intimate meetings such as coffee with a close friend or a small group supper. Each time, she focused on confronting and reframing her negative thoughts in a more positive light.

For example, when her mind wandered to thoughts like *They're all criticizing me*, Sarah would reply with *I don't know what others are thinking, and they're probably more interested in having fun than studying me.* Sarah eventually regained her confidence in social situations as she made these small movements.

Practical Strategies for Overcoming Social Anxiety

Sarah's path highlights the importance of taking small, doable steps to overcome social anxiety. While it may appear to be a daunting task, there are several methods that can assist individuals in managing their anxiety and feeling more at ease in social situations:

1. Challenge Negative Ideas: Social anxiety typically manifests as a flood of negative thoughts about how others perceive you. The goal is to identify these ideas and actively challenge them. Instead of thinking that everyone is judging you, remember that most people are too involved with their own lives to scrutinize everything you say or do.

2. Start with Small Exposures: Avoiding circumstances just increases anxiety. To break the cycle, start by gradually exposing yourself to social situations that generate anxiety. Begin with low-pressure situations, such as talking to the clerk or meeting a buddy for coffee. As your confidence improves, you can progress to bigger tournaments.

3. Mindfulness techniques might help you be present in the moment rather than being preoccupied with worrying thoughts. Deep breathing exercises, grounding techniques, or simply focusing on your surroundings can all assist in reducing the physical symptoms of anxiety.

4. Plan Ahead of Time: If you're attending an event that makes you nervous, come up with some conversation openers or questions ahead of time. Having a strategy may help you relax and concentrate.

5. Set Realistic Expectations: Remember that no one is perfect, and social interactions do not need to be flawless. Allow yourself to make mistakes, and remember that embarrassing circumstances happen to everyone.

6. Seek Help: Talking to a therapist or visiting a support group can be therapeutic and offer a safe space to discuss your concerns.

The Road to Confidence

Sarah's concern gradually subsided. She was still nervous in some social situations, but she no longer let her fears control her conduct. She was able to enjoy social occasions in ways she hadn't in years by progressively exposing herself to different situations, questioning her negative ideas, and practicing self-compassion.

Her goal wasn't to become a social butterfly or attend every party; it was to get the courage to interact with others on her own terms. Sarah's social anxiety was always present, but it no longer dictated her actions.

Professional help can provide you with particular strategies for dealing with your social anxiety.

4.

Managing Depression

"Depression may cloud your path, but with the right support and small steps forward, you can find your way through the fog and reclaim your light."

Relatable Story

James awakened to the sound of his alarm, just like every other day, but today seemed different. He stared at the ceiling, his body heavy with an imaginary weight. Getting out of bed and starting the day seemed like a huge task. He rolled over, pulled the covers over his head, and hit the snooze button. Again. And again.

It wasn't that James lacked things to do; he had plenty. There was a job to go to, errands to run, and friends who had tried to contact me—but none of it felt significant anymore. The joy he used to derive from simple things like playing his guitar or going for a run had disappeared, leaving him in a state of numbness. He couldn't pinpoint when it began, but over weeks and months, his energy, motivation, and zest for life had dwindled.

Depression had slowly crept into James' life, but it was tenacious. It sapped his energy, depressed his emotions, and made each day feel like a laborious climb up a slippery hill. James did not want to feel this way; he missed the guy he used to be, the one who smiled readily and found joy in the most mundane things. But for now, he was lost in the darkness, wondering how to return.

Understanding Depression

Depression is more than just sadness or dejection. A persistent, overwhelming sensation of pessimism and exhaustion pervades all areas of a person's existence. People who are depressed may struggle to complete everyday tasks, experience joy, or even get out of bed in the morning. It may feel like a fog over the mind and body, making even the simplest chores appear difficult.

Some common symptoms of depression include:

- Persistent feelings of sadness, emptiness, or hopelessness

- Loss of interest or pleasure in activities once enjoyed

- Fatigue or lack of energy

- Difficulty concentrating or making decisions

- Changes in sleep patterns (insomnia or excessive sleeping)

- Changes in appetite or weight

- Feelings of worthlessness or guilt

- Thoughts of death or suicide

For James, depression manifested as a loss of motivation and energy. Things he formerly enjoyed—his profession, his passions, his relationships—now felt like burdens. He couldn't see any way out, and the longer he stayed in this state, the more isolated and alienated he felt.

James' Path to Managing Depression

After several weeks of laboring alone, James had reached his breaking point. He had missed work for three days in a row, unable to generate the energy to get out of bed. His pals had noticed his isolation, and one evening, after ignoring a string of texts from his best friend, he heard a tap on the door. James reluctantly opened it, only to find his friend standing there with a worried expression.

"You don't have to say anything," his friend said gently, "but I'm here. And I'm not going anywhere."

Something changed for James at that precise moment. He realized he didn't have to confront this fight alone. His friend's presence gave him hope that, despite his sorrow, there were people who cared about him.

That night, James told his friend that he had been struggling for months, unable to overcome the enormous emotion that had consumed his life. His friend listened without judgment and encouraged James to seek professional help.

James made an appointment with a therapist the next day with the assistance of a buddy. It was not a straightforward step, but it was necessary. In therapy, James found that depression was not a sign of weakness or failure, but rather a physical ailment that required treatment and care.

Practical Strategies for Managing Depression

James' journey emphasizes the importance of seeking help and taking action to overcome depression. While it cannot be "fixed" overnight, there are strategies that can help people cope and recover control of their lives.

1. Seek Support: Depression thrives in isolation. Seek help from your friends, family, or a mental health professional.

Talking about your feelings can be very healing since it reminds you that you are not alone.

2. Establish a Routine: Depression may make even the simplest chores appear onerous. Creating a daily routine can provide structure and a sense of purpose. Begin with modest, manageable goals—getting out of bed, showering, eating a meal—and work your way up from there.

3. Exercise and Physical Activity: Physical activity can be an excellent way to manage depression. While it may appear impossible to exercise when you are unhappy, even a short walk or some gentle stretching can boost your mood by releasing endorphins, the brain's natural feel-good chemicals.

4. Mindfulness and meditation practices, such as deep breathing exercises, can help you stay present and reduce the negative thoughts that often accompany melancholy. These tactics can also aid in emotional regulation and stress reduction.

5. Challenge Negative Thoughts: Depression can cause a flood of negative thoughts, such as feelings of worthlessness or hopelessness. Cognitive-behavioral therapy (CBT) encourages people to evaluate their beliefs and replace them with more balanced, positive ones. Instead of thinking *I'm useless*, try reframing it as *I'm suffering right now, but I'm working to improve*.

6. Seek Professional Help: Depression is a medical problem that frequently necessitates professional intervention, such as therapy or medication. Therapists can help you create coping techniques that are suited to your individual situation, while medication can help address chemical imbalances in the brain that lead to depression.

7. Be Kind to Yourself: Healing from depression takes time, so practice self-compassion throughout. Instead of blaming yourself for what you haven't accomplished, focus on tiny accomplishments and acknowledge your attempts to improve.

The Road to Recovery

For James, therapy was a lifeline. He eventually acquired coping mechanisms to manage his melancholy, and with the help of his therapist, he began to take small steps toward reintegration into life. He started with small walks, reconnected with friends, and gradually resumed activities he used to like, such as playing guitar.

While there were some difficult days, James no longer felt like he was sinking into quicksand. He had a support system in place, including a therapist who understood his issues and abilities to assist him get through difficult moments. Depression remained in his life, but he was no longer its prisoner.

Depression recovery is an up-and-down process. However, with the right help and skills, it is possible to overcome sadness and reclaim a sense of purpose and meaning in life.

5.

Battling Chronic Stress

"Chronic stress may feel like a constant weight, but with clear boundaries and self-care, you can lift the burden and reclaim control over your life."

Sophia was recognized for her ability to manage multiple projects at once. As a project manager at a fast-paced technology company, she was constantly on the go, responding to emails, attending meetings, and making sure deadlines were reached. Her calendar was packed with back-to-back appointments, and her phone was constantly ringing with notifications. Sophia took pride in her productivity and stress-management abilities until she couldn't anymore.

It began with headaches. Nothing serious, just a dull pain that she could treat with some medication. Then began the sleepless nights. Sophia woke up at 2 a.m., her mind racing through an infinite to-do list. She was exhausted, but sleep wouldn't come. Her body quickly began to communicate more symptoms, such as muscle tightness, gastrointestinal problems, irritability, and an overwhelming sense of dread every time she opened her laptop.

Sophia thought she could handle it. After all, everyone in her line of work faced stress, right? However, the stress finally took a toll on both her mental and physical health. She started making mistakes at work, forgetting things, and yelling at her colleagues. Her vitality was spent, and she no longer felt in control of her situation.

The breaking point came one morning when she found herself crying in her car before leaving for work. Sophia sat in the parking lot, hands gripping the steering wheel, unable to move herself inside the building. She felt trapped—trapped by her responsibilities, expectations, and the weight of the chronic stress she had been suffering from for months.

Sophia's story isn't rare. Chronic stress, if not managed, can gradually erode a person's well-being, resulting in burnout, physical health problems, and mental health difficulties. In today's fast-paced world, when we are constantly linked and expected to perform, stress management is more important than ever.

Understanding Chronic Stress

Stress is a natural reaction to challenging situations, and in moderation, it may be motivating and even beneficial. However, when stress becomes chronic—that is, it persists for an extended period of time without relief—it can have serious consequences for both physical and mental health.

Chronic stress activates the body's fight-or-flight response, releasing cortisol and adrenaline. While this response is advantageous in short-term situations (such as times of danger), prolonged exposure to these stress hormones can be harmful to the body. It could lead to:

- Increased risk of heart disease

- High blood pressure

- Weakened immune system

- Digestive problems

- Insomnia

- Anxiety and depression

Sophia was on the edge of burnout from the continual stress of her demanding career. She was experiencing physical and emotional symptoms of stress overload, which was impacting her mental health.

Sophia's Path to Battling Chronic Stress

Sophia's car broke down, which acted as a wake-up call. She realized she couldn't continue at her current rate without serious consequences to her health. That afternoon, she contacted her boss and requested a week off to focus on her health.

Sophia focused on her personal well-being that week. She began by contacting a therapist who specializes in stress management. Sophia began to understand the underlying causes of her stress and learned appropriate coping mechanisms during therapy.

One of the first lessons she learned was the importance of setting boundaries. Sophia had always said "yes" to every opportunity, request, and responsibility that came her way. She did, however, practice saying "no" when she noticed her plate was full. She also started distributing tasks to her team members rather than attempting to do everything alone.

Sophia also learned how to disengage from her job. She'd fallen into the trap of being always available, checking emails late at night, and responding to messages on her days off. Sophia, with the help of her therapist, established a rule for herself: no work after 6 p.m., and no email checking on weekends. This boundary enabled her to recharge and reconnect with her personal life, which she had neglected for far too long.

Practical Strategies for Managing Chronic Stress.

Sophia's journey to stress management stresses the need to make intentional changes in how we approach work and daily life. Here are some practical approaches to reducing chronic stress:

1. Set Clear Boundaries: One of the most common causes of chronic stress is an inability to separate work and personal life. It is vital to set limits between professional and personal time. This could include setting strict "office hours," turning off email notifications after a certain time or learning to say "no" to new responsibilities when you're already overburdened.

2. Practice Mindfulness and Relaxation: Mindfulness techniques such as meditation, deep breathing exercises, and yoga can assist in calming the mind and reduce the physiological effects of stress. Taking even five minutes out of your day to concentrate on your breathing can have a significant effect.

3. Prioritize Self-Care: When stress sets in, self-care is often the first thing to go. However, it is vital to set aside time for things that nourish both your mind and body, such as exercise, spending time with loved ones, or engaging in a hobby you enjoy.

4. Delegate and Ask for Help: You do not have to do everything yourself. Delegating responsibility to others and seeking support when necessary might help lessen the overwhelming pressure to succeed. Sophia learned that by distributing the workload among her coworkers, she was able to focus on what was most important without burning out.

5. Manage Your Time Effectively: Chronic stress is frequently created by the sense that there is too much to accomplish and insufficient time to complete it. Time management techniques such as creating to-do lists, prioritizing activities, and breaking down work into smaller portions can help you stay organized and less overwhelmed.

6. Seek Professional Help: If chronic stress is impacting your mental and physical health, speaking with a therapist or counselor can be life-changing. A mental health professional can help you establish personalized stress management strategies and coping skills.

The Road to Recovery

Sophia noticed a difference as she began to implement these adjustments in her life. She no longer felt overwhelmed by her responsibilities. Her stress levels began to decrease and she regained her sense of equilibrium. She still had challenging days, but she now had the tools to deal with them without allowing stress to overwhelm her.

Sophia's story tells us that persistent stress is not to be underestimated. It signifies that something in our lives must alter. We may avoid burnout and protect our emotional and physical health by managing stress, creating boundaries, and putting self-care first.

Chronic stress is common in today's fast-paced environment, but it doesn't have to control your life. With the right strategies and support, you may regain your sense of serenity, balance, and well-being.

Part2:
Confronting
Internal Struggles

6.

The Loneliness of Grief

"Grief may isolate us in the beginning but through connection, vulnerability, and time, we discover that we are never truly alone in our sorrow."

Relatable Story

Sarah never imagined how empty her life would be after losing her mother. It was as if the environment had suddenly gone quieter, but her mind was as active as ever. The daily phone talks, the shared laughter, and the simple understanding that someone was always there for her were all gone in an instant.

People first came together to support her. Friends donated food, and flowers, and checked in to make sure she was all right. However, as the weeks and months passed, the number of calls and visits declined. Everyone else's life went on, but Sarah felt trapped by her loss, alone in her grief.

She attempted to express her emotions, but no one seemed to understand. She received messages like "It'll get better with time" and so on. "Stay strong, your mother wouldn't want you to be sad." Though everyone meant well, these words only added to her feelings of loneliness. How could she be strong when she felt so broken? And how could time ever heal the grief of losing someone so deeply?

Sarah realized that grief is a deeply personal experience that can make people feel lonely and alone. When the first shock of loss subsides and the world moves on, the loneliness of mourning can set in, exacerbating an already difficult situation.

Understanding the Loneliness of Grief

Grief is a natural response to loss, but many people are unaware that it is frequently accompanied by profound feelings of loneliness. Loneliness can come from a variety of sources:

1. The Physical Absence of a Loved One: The most evident cause of loneliness is the death of a loved one. Their presence, talks, and company are no longer in your life, creating a painful void.

2. The Feeling of Misunderstanding: Even when others offer assistance, mourners frequently feel misunderstood. Well-intended counsel or platitudes such as "time heals all wounds" may unintentionally reduce the sadness of loss, leaving the bereaved individual feeling even more isolated.

3. The World Moves On: After a loss, there may be an outpouring of compassion from friends and family. However, as time passes, people typically return to their normal occupations, leaving the bereaved person to deal with their emotions alone. This can intensify feelings of loneliness since it looks like the rest of the world has forgotten about your loss, while you continue to suffer.

4. Internalized grief: Some people may feel forced to "stay strong" or ignore their emotions, so they bottle up their sadness. As a result, people may feel lonely because they can't openly express their pain to others.

Sarah experienced all of these sorts of loneliness. She mourned her mother deeply, felt misunderstood by others around her, and watched the world go by while she stayed locked in her grief. Each day felt like an uphill battle, and her sorrow worsened as the loneliness set in.

Sarah's Journey to Healing

Sarah struggled to deal with her grief and isolation in the months after her mother died. However, she eventually learned that, while loss would never go away, there are ways to lessen loneliness and start the healing process.

One of the first things Sarah did was allow herself to fully experience her emotions. For months, she tried to be tough, hiding her pain and pretending everything was well. However, this made her feel even more distant from herself and others. Finally, she realized it was okay to freely mourn, weep, miss her mother, and express her anguish. In doing so, she permitted herself to begin healing.

Sarah also reached out to people who had experienced similar events. She joined a grief support group and met people who understood what she was going through. She didn't need to explain or justify her unhappiness in this situation because everyone else had been there before. This sense of connection enabled her to overcome the loneliness that had been weighing her down.

Practical Strategies to Cope with Grief-related Loneliness

Grief may be a solitary experience, but there are ways to combat the loneliness that often accompanies it.

1. Allow Yourself to Grieve: Allowing yourself to feel your emotions is one of the most important steps toward overcoming grief's loneliness. Suppressing your feelings

only makes you feel more alone. Accepting your loss and admitting your pain is the first step towards healing.

2. Seek Support from Others Who Understand: Grief support groups, whether in person or online, can provide a great deal of comfort. Connecting with others who have experienced loss can help ease the sense of being misunderstood and remind you that you are not alone.

3. Maintain Connections with Loved Ones: While remaining in touch with friends and family during a time of grief might be difficult, it can help combat loneliness. Even if they don't fully understand what you're going through, their presence can be soothing and encouraging.

4. Create a Ritual to Honor Your Loved One: Creating a meaningful ritual to remember your loved one can help fill the emptiness left by their death. Whether it's lighting a candle, visiting a favorite spot, or simply reflecting on their memories, these rituals can provide a sense of connection and peace.

5. Consider Professional Support: If the loneliness of grieving overwhelms you, speaking with a therapist or counselor may help. A professional can help you understand the complexity of loss.

Moving Forward with Hope.

As Sarah worked through her grief, she discovered that, while the loneliness of loss is never totally gone, it can be managed with time and effort. She still missed her mother every day, but she sought ways to reconnect with her memories while relying on the support of people around her.

Grief is a process that can be approached in various ways. However, by allowing yourself to feel your emotions, seeking treatment, and finding ways to honor your loved one, you can start to feel less lonely and go forward with hope.

7

The Trap of Perfectionism

"Perfectionism is the thief of joy, a trap that keeps us chasing an illusion. True success lies not in being flawless, but in the courage to be imperfect and still move forward."

Anna was a natural perfectionist with a strong determination. She excelled in academics, sports, and music from a young age, and she was constantly praised for her dedication and impeccable accomplishments. Everyone around her saw her as the embodiment of success. Despite her triumphs, Anna was always nervous and anxious.

Every task she engaged in had to be accomplished correctly. Anna would spend hours perfecting every detail of a professional job, cooking dinner for friends, or keeping her house clean. Even the most minor blunder felt like a failure, and she couldn't forgive herself for it. She was constantly tweaking, editing, and reworking things long after others believed they were "good enough".

Nonetheless, the pursuit of perfection was demanding. No matter how hard she tried, Anna couldn't shake the feeling that she wasn't meeting her own high standards, let alone the expectations of others. The more she strived for perfection, the more concerned she grew, until she was fatigued and overwhelmed by even the most basic tasks.

Anna ultimately realized that her perfectionism was impeding her progress rather than assisting it. It triggered a loop of anxiety, fear of failure, and a sense of never being good enough. Even while others praised her accomplishments, Anna felt shackled by her high standards, unable to appreciate any of her victories.

Understanding Perfectionism

Perfectionism, while often considered a strength, maybe a double-edged weapon. On the surface, perfectionism appears to be the pursuit of greatness, but it often masks deeper issues of insecurity, fear of failure, and a desire for control. For many people, like Anna, the desire to be perfect becomes a trap, resulting in mental health difficulties such as worry, sadness, and weariness.

Perfectionism is defined by the desire to meet impossibly high standards. These norms, whether self-imposed or assumed to derive from external sources, create great pressure. Perfectionists are often self-critical, believing that nothing they do is ever good enough, even if it meets or exceeds others' expectations.

There are different forms of perfectionism:

1. Self-Oriented Perfectionism: This involves establishing unrealistic goals for oneself and being harshly critical of one's own performance.

2. Other-Oriented Perfectionism: In this situation, the individual expects others to meet impossible high standards and may be judgmental if they do not.

3. Socially Prescribed Perfectionism: In this variant, people believe that others expect them to be perfect and are under intense pressure to meet these perceived standards.

While pursuing excellence is not inherently undesirable, perfectionism is distinguished by an all-or-nothing attitude. Perfectionists see everything less than perfection as a failure, and their black-and-white thinking may make life seem burdensome and dreary.

Anna's Journey to Letting Go

Anna sensed that something had to change. She was upset by the constant strain and realized that her perfectionism was robbing her of happiness. The first step in her journey was acknowledging that perfectionism was not a healthy motivator, but rather a source of stress that kept her from enjoying life.

Her journey to overcome perfectionism was not easy, but it was transformative. One of the first things Anna did was redefine success. Instead of comparing herself to unattainable goals, she chose to value progress over perfection. Completing a task, even if it is not flawless, is an achievement to be proud of.

Anna also learned to embrace vulnerability. One of her main motivations for perfectionism was a fear of failure and judgment. However, through therapy and the support of friends, she learned that flaws and shortcomings were an unavoidable part of being human. Sharing her struggles, rather than hiding behind a veneer of perfection, enabled her to develop deeper, more honest relationships with others.

Practical Strategies for Overcoming Perfectionism

Overcoming perfectionism needs a mental shift and an acceptance of shortcomings. Here are some practical methods to help:

1. Face perfectionistic thoughts. If you find yourself thinking, "This has to be perfect," or "I can't make any mistakes," challenge those thoughts. Consider the following questions: "What's the worst that could happen if it's not perfect?" or "Would I judge someone else this harshly?"

2. Set realistic goals. Instead of striving for perfection, prioritize development. Set reasonable goals and recognize that doing anything properly is preferable to doing nothing at all out of fear of failure.

3. Practice Self-Compassion: Be kind to yourself when you make mistakes or fall short of your goals. Self-compassion allows you to learn and grow from challenges rather than becoming paralyzed by them.

4. Break Down Tasks Into Smaller Steps: Perfectionism sometimes leads to procrastination because the task at hand appears too difficult. Break down large tasks into smaller, more manageable steps, and focus on completing one at a time.

5. Learn to Accept Good Enough: Remember that everything does not have to be perfect. Often, "good enough" suffices to complete the work. Getting rid of the desire for perfection can lower stress and increase productivity.

6. Seek Support: Perfectionism can be deeply rooted in past experiences or personal insecurities. Talking to a therapist or counselor can help you discover the underlying causes of your perfectionism and develop appropriate coping strategies.

Moving Forward with a Healthier Mindset

Anna's effort to overcome perfectionism did not include lowering her standards or abandoning her goals. Instead, it was about creating a balance, understanding that aiming for excellence is not synonymous with wanting perfection. Anna learned that embracing imperfection enabled her to achieve great things while alleviating the terrible pressure and self-criticism that had previously held her back.

Anna realized that letting go of perfectionism made life more enjoyable. She had more energy, less anxiety, and a stronger sense of purpose in her personal and professional lives. The trap of perfectionism had once made her feel small and inadequate, but Anna found release by recognizing her humanity, flaws, and all.

8

Confronting Self-Esteem Issues

"True self-esteem is not about perfection or comparison; it's about recognizing your worth, embracing your flaws, and knowing that you are enough just as you are."

Regardless of where he was, James always felt out of place. At work, he questioned his abilities, convinced that his peers were superior, wiser, and more skilled. At social gatherings, he felt invisible, as if no one wanted to interact with him. He tried to blend in, but he had the sensation that he wasn't good enough.

Growing up, James' parents had great expectations for him yet rarely complimented him. Instead, they emphasized how he could have done better. When he brought home good grades, they would wonder why he hadn't gotten higher grades. If he won a sporting event, they would point out his mistakes. Over time, James grew to believe that no matter what he did, nothing would be adequate. This mindset followed him into adulthood, where his low self-esteem began to undermine every aspect of his life, including his work and relationships.

He hesitated to take praises, either ignoring them or convincing himself that they were just being nice. Even when he accomplished something major, such as a promotion at work, he felt like an imposter, constantly fearful that someone would discover he was not as capable as they had assumed.

Self-doubt overcame James. He was continually comparing himself to others and seeking methods to better. The more he focused on his perceived defects, the lower his self-esteem grew. He felt imprisoned in a loop of self-criticism and negative thinking, and no matter what he did, he couldn't get rid of the sensation that he wasn't good enough.

Understanding Self-Esteem Issues

Self-esteem is the foundation of how we see ourselves, our worth, and our abilities. When we have high self-esteem, we recognize our talents while also embracing our imperfections. However, low self-esteem can distort our image of ourselves, leading us to believe that we are less capable, desirable, and deserving of happiness than others.

Low self-esteem often develops over time, impacted by life experiences, relationships, and personal beliefs. James's childhood feelings of inadequacy contributed to his low self-esteem in adulthood. Trauma, bullying, failure, and negative self-talk can all cause poor self-esteem.

Common signs of low self-esteem include:

1. Constant Self-Criticism: People with low self-esteem typically engage in harsh self-criticism, highlighting their flaws and errors while downplaying their strengths and accomplishments.

2. Fear of Failure: A lack of confidence in one's abilities can lead to an overwhelming fear of failure. This anxiety may lead to procrastination, avoidance, or abandonment of goals entirely.

3. Difficult Accepting praise: People with low self-esteem may struggle to accept praise, believing it is useless or dismissing it as fake.

4. Comparison with Others: People with low self-esteem often compare themselves to others, leading to feelings of inadequacy and self-doubt.

5. Imposter Syndrome: The belief that one's accomplishments are undeserved and that they are a fraud, despite evidence to the contrary.

6. People-Pleasing Behavior: People with low self-esteem may go out of their way to please others, looking for external validation to feel valued.

Low self-esteem can be immensely harmful to mental health, creating anxiety, sadness, and a diminished sense of self-worth. James's continual belief that he wasn't good enough hampered his own growth and satisfaction.

James's Journey to Rebuilding Self-Esteem

James realized that something needed to change. He was tired of continuously doubting himself and feeling insecure. With the help of a therapist, he began to confront the deeply held beliefs that had been holding him back for so long.

The first step in James' journey was admitting that his self-esteem issues did not define him. He felt unworthy, but that did not imply he was. This distinction allowed James to separate his emotions from reality and begin combating the bad beliefs that had previously dominated his life.

One of James' most effective exercises was substituting negative self talk with positive affirmations. When he found himself thinking "I'm not good enough" or "I'll never succeed," he made a concentrated effort to replace those thoughts with affirmations such as "I am capable" and "I deserve success." It looked awkward and forced at first, but James noticed a shift in his self-perception with time.

James also practiced accepting praise. Instead of ignoring compliments, he learned to say, "Thank you," and truly appreciate positive feedback. By allowing himself to receive compliments, James discovered that others viewed him far more positively than he did himself.

Practical Strategies for Confronting Self-Esteem Issues

Building self-esteem is a process that takes time, but it is possible to change how you view yourself. Here are some practical strategies for confronting self-esteem issues:

1. Challenge Negative Self-Talk: Consider how you speak with yourself. Are your opinions too critical or harsh? When you notice yourself engaged in negative self-talk, question it by asking, "Is this true?" Then replace it with more realistic, positive comments.

2. Practice Self-Compassion: Treat yourself with the same respect and understanding as you would a friend. When you make a mistake or feel like you've failed, remember that everyone has flaws and shortcomings, and they don't lessen your worth.

3. Set Achievable Goals. Start by setting small, attainable goals. Every accomplishment, no matter how minor,

contributes to a greater sense of competence and confidence.

4. Stop comparing yourself to others: Remember that each person's experience is unique. Constant comparison with others will only weaken your self-esteem. Instead of comparing yourself to others, concentrate on your own accomplishments and development.

5. Accept Compliments: If someone compliments you, don't discount or disregard it. Simply say "Thank you," and let yourself absorb the positive feedback.

6. Seek Help: Speaking with a therapist or counselor can help you uncover the underlying causes of your low self-esteem and provide strategies for rebuilding your sense of self-worth.

Moving Forward with Greater Self-Worth

James' route to regaining his self-esteem was challenging but worthwhile. He eventually silenced his inner critic, who had been dominating his life for years. He began to take pride in his accomplishments and felt himself capable and deserving of pleasure.

Building self-esteem takes time, but with perseverance and practice, you can develop a healthier, more positive self-image. The key is to understand that self-worth is not determined by accomplishments, external praise, or comparisons to others—it comes from within.

9.

Overcoming Imposter Syndrome

"Success is not an accident, and you are not a fraud. You are deserving of your achievements, not because of luck, but because of your hard work, talent, and perseverance."

Relatable Story

Sophia sat at her desk, looking at the computer's bright screen, her heart beating. She had recently been elevated to a senior marketing position at her company, a goal she had been working toward for years. Rather than celebrating, she became gripped with anxiety. Her mind raced with thoughts such as, "They made a mistake." I am not qualified for this. They will learn that I am not as smart as they believe I am.

Sophia couldn't shake the sensation that she didn't deserve her success, even though her team's projects were always meeting or exceeding their objectives, and she had been recognized multiple times for her original ideas. Deep down, she believed she had just been lucky, and that everyone would soon see her for what she was: a fraud.

Sophia's overwhelming sense of self-doubt went beyond her professional life. She was cautious to express her opinions at meetings for fear of appearing incompetent. When she received compliments from her coworkers, she dismissed them, assuming they were only being kind. Even at home, she fought to unwind, always feeling the need to establish her worth.

Sophia was suffering from imposter syndrome, a psychological condition in which people question their accomplishments and fear being exposed as a "fraud." This internalized belief that success is unearned can impede even the most successful people from fully appreciating their successes.

Understanding Imposter Syndrome

Imposter syndrome is more common than you know. It affects people from a variety of backgrounds, including students, professionals, artists, and even highly skilled leaders. It's the feeling that you've duped others into thinking you're capable, and it's only a matter of time before they realize you don't fit in. Even if you have proof of your accomplishments, imposter syndrome convinces you that you are unqualified for success.

There are a few key characteristics of imposter syndrome:

1. Doubting Your Competence: Regardless of how much you've accomplished, imposter syndrome causes you to believe that you don't deserve your success. You may believe you are not as capable as others say you are, and that your success is the result of luck rather than competence.

2. Fear of Being Exposed: People suffering from impostor syndrome are constantly afraid that others will "find out" they are not as brilliant or capable as they appear. This concern can cause anxiety, stress, and perfectionism as they attempt to conceal their perceived flaws.

3. Attributing achievement to External variables: Instead of acknowledging your hard work and talent, impostor syndrome causes you to attribute your achievement to variables outside your control, such as luck, timing, or even someone else's assistance.

4. Perfectionism: People suffering from imposter syndrome tend to set unreasonable high standards for themselves, worrying that any slip-up will reveal their perceived inadequacies.

Imposter syndrome can afflict anyone, but it is most prevalent among high achievers. The paradox is that when you achieve greater success, you may assume you do not deserve it. Sophia's feelings of inadequacy increased with each promotion and reward. She felt caught in a continuous loop of striving for perfection, convinced that nothing she did would ever be enough.

Sophia's Journey to Overcoming Imposter Syndrome

Sophia felt she couldn't keep living in constant fear of being "found out." With the help of her mentor, she started the tough but necessary process of conquering imposter syndrome.

The first step was to recognize that her emotions were genuine but not grounded in truth. Her mentor helped her see that her success was due to her hard work and talent, not luck or dishonesty. This realization was critical for Sophia because it enabled her to begin resisting the negative thoughts that had been dominating her life.

Sophia then started charting her accomplishments. Every time she received praise or achieved a goal, she noted it. Over time, she compiled a concrete record of her accomplishments, serving as a reminder that she was capable and deserving of success. This action helped her overcome the inner voice that told her she didn't belong.

Sophia also learned to share her feelings with trusted coworkers and friends. She was astounded to discover that many of them had experienced similar feelings of inadequacy. By discussing her problems, she realized that imposter syndrome thrives in isolation, and the more she expressed it, the less effect it had on her.

Finally, Sophia attempted to suppress her inner critic. She practiced self-compassion, reminding herself that nobody is perfect and that making mistakes does not lessen her worth. When she sensed herself slipping into self-doubt, she would pause, take a deep breath, and remind herself of her accomplishments and abilities.

Practical Strategies for Overcoming Imposter Syndrome

Overcoming imposter syndrome isn't easy, but it is possible. Here are some strategies to help you break free from the cycle of self-doubt and embrace your achievements:

1. Acknowledge Your Feelings: Recognizing the presence of imposter syndrome is the first step toward resolving it. Understand that your feelings of inadequacy are not an accurate reflection of your abilities, but rather the outcome of self-doubt.

2. Reframe Negative beliefs: Address the negative beliefs that cause imposter syndrome. When you find yourself thinking, "I don't deserve this," replace it with more positive, realistic thoughts, such as, "I've worked hard for this, and I deserve my success."

3. Document Your Achievements: Keep track of all your successes, no matter how big or small. This might be as simple as documenting a compliment you received at work

or a project you successfully completed. Over time, this list will serve as evidence of your accomplishments.

4. Stop comparing yourself to others: Everyone's journey is unique. Avoid comparing your hidden problems to others' visible accomplishments. Instead of comparing yourself to others, focus on your own personal growth and development.

5. Accept appreciation: When someone appreciates you, resist the urge to downplay or dismiss it. Practice saying "thank you," and allow yourself to absorb positive feedback.

6. Seek Support: Don't be afraid to talk about your feelings with a trusted mentor, colleague, or therapist. Often, simply voicing your feelings can help reduce the tension of being alone.

7. Practice Self-Compassion: Be gentle to yourself. Remember that everyone makes mistakes, and nobody is perfect. Treat yourself with the same compassion and understanding that you would extend to a friend.

Moving Forward with Confidence

Sophia's road was difficult, but by recognizing her emotions, questioning her negative ideas, and getting help, she was able to overcome the imposter syndrome that had held her back for so long. She recognized that achievement should be celebrated and enjoyed rather than feared or embarrassed of.

If you've ever felt like an imposter in your own life, remember that you're not alone. Many people, regardless of accomplishment, experience comparable sentiments at some point. However, by tackling your anxieties and acknowledging your own worth, you may overcome impostor syndrome and move forward with confidence and self-esteem.

10.

The Struggle with Body Image

"Your body is not the measure of your worth. It's the vessel that carries you through life, and it deserves love, care, and respect, no matter how it looks."

Relatable Story

Olivia stood in front of her bedroom mirror, ripping at her clothes in frustration, on a typical Saturday afternoon. The pants she had loved just a few months ago now felt tight around her waist, and every outfit she tried seemed to highlight the parts of her body she loathed the most. Her reflection was foreign and harsh.

Scrolling around social media simply made her feelings worse. She saw many photos of toned, thin ladies posing easily in nicely styled ensembles. The comparison game began, and as she swiped, a sickening feeling of inadequacy set in. *Why can't I look like that?' she wondered. Everyone else seemed to know the secret to being beautiful, but Olivia felt stuck, unable to meet the unattainable expectations she was constantly assaulted with.

Olivia was accustomed to these feelings. She has suffered from body image issues since she was a child. Despite being active and healthy, she was constantly dissatisfied with her appearance. She was constantly self-conscious about her arms, tummy, and legs. The constant battle with self-criticism was tiring, and Olivia had no idea how to stop.

Understanding Body Image

Body image refers to how we perceive our own body and believe others see us. It is not just about how we appear physically, but also about how we perceive and feel about our appearance. Accepting and appreciating your body for who it is, warts and all, is the first step toward a healthy body image. However, when someone struggles with body image, such as Olivia, it can lead to a mistaken view of their body, eliciting feelings of guilt, anxiety, and even self-loathing.

The problem of body image is widespread. Society constantly promotes rigid and often unrealistic beauty standards, particularly through media and advertising. People who do not fit into these idealized models may feel inadequate as a result of the pressure. It's easy to forget that the images we see, whether in advertising, movies, or social media, are frequently heavily edited and managed. Despite this, the comparison trap can leave us feeling inadequate.

There are several ways in which negative body image can manifest:

1. Constant criticism of appearances: People who battle with body image may continually scrutinize their appearances, pointing out issues that others may miss. This criticism is usually focused on weight, skin, hair, and other physical characteristics.

2. Unhealthy Comparison: People with body image concerns typically compare themselves to others, particularly images from the media. These comparisons frequently make people feel inferior.

3. Disordered Eating and Exercise Habits: To "correct" perceived shortcomings, some people may form unhealthy addictions to food or exercise. In an attempt to conform to

societal expectations, people may indulge in disordered eating, excessive activity, or crash dieting.

4. Avoidance of Social Events: People with low body image may avoid social events in which they believe their appearance will be scrutinized. They may turn down invites to parties, the beach, or other events for fear of having their bodies scrutinized.

5. Mental Health Effects: Constant stress from feeling inadequate can harm mental health, causing anxiety, depression, and feelings of isolation.

Olivia's Path to Healing

Olivia recognized she couldn't keep living in the cycle of self-criticism. It affected her self-esteem, social life, and physical health. She thought it was time to take action and modify her perspective on body image, even if she didn't know where to start. Olivia worked with a therapist to progressively change her perspective on her body and learn how to have a healthier, more positive connection with it.

The first step was to recognize that her worth was unconnected to her looks. Olivia's therapist helped her recognize that she was more than her body—she was a kind, bright, and accomplished woman whose qualities had nothing to do with the size of her trousers. This change in viewpoint was essential for Olivia. It enabled her to divorce her feeling of worth from her physical appearance.

Olivia then focused on reframing negative thoughts about her body. When she caught herself criticizing her appearance, she would pause and try to replace the thought with something more compassionate. For example, if she caught herself thinking, "My stomach looks dreadful today," she would try to reframe it as, "My body allows me to move, work, and enjoy life, which is something to be grateful for.

Olivia also made a conscious effort to curate her social media feed. She unfollowed accounts that promoted unrealistic beauty standards and began following body-positive influencers who promoted diversity and self-esteem. This shift enabled Olivia to see a wider range of body shapes and realize that beauty comes in many forms.

Olivia's therapy involved learning to listen to her body. Rather than forcing herself to stick to rigorous diets or fitness routines, she focused on nurturing her body in a way that felt healthy and sustainable. She learned to eat intuitively and exercise for the joy of movement rather than as a punishment for her appearance.

Finally, Olivia surrounded herself with people who promoted positive body image. She began to open up to her close friends about her problems, and they replied with empathy and encouragement. Knowing she wasn't alone on her path increased her confidence immensely.

Overcoming Body Image Struggles

If you, like Olivia, struggle with body image, here are some suggestions to help you create a healthier relationship with your body:

1. Practice Self-Compassion: Rather than criticizing your appearance, treat yourself with respect. Recognize that no one is perfect, and value your body for what it allows you to do.

2. Challenge Unrealistic Beauty Standards: Keep in mind that images in the media are frequently manipulated and may not accurately reflect reality. Challenge the concept that there is just one "right" way to look, and appreciate the variety of beauty.

3. Focus on What Your Body Can Do, Not How It Looks: Shift your emphasis from beauty to utility. Appreciate your body's skills, whether they involve running, dancing, or simply allowing you to enjoy life.

4. Surround Yourself with Positivity: Pay attention to the messages you get, especially on social media. Follow accounts that promote body positivity and self-acceptance.

5. Seek Professional Help: If negative body image is affecting your mental health, see a therapist. They can help you navigate the emotional problems associated with body image issues and provide you with coping strategies.

6. Celebrate Small Victories: Every step toward a healthier body image is important. Celebrate your accomplishments, whether by wearing comfy clothing or reframing a negative perspective.

Moving Forward with Self-Acceptance

Olivia's path to accepting her body was not swift; it took time, patience, and a lot of self-reflection. However, with each minor victory, she began to see her body as a separate part of herself, rather than something to be reviled. She found that a dress size or a number on the scale does not determine one's self-worth. It is visible in how we treat ourselves, how we care for our bodies, and how we choose to see the beauty in our own reflection.

Part 3: Navigating External Pressures

11.

The Burden of Burnout

"Burnout is not a badge of honor; it's a signal that something needs to change. You can't pour from an empty cup, so take care of yourself first."

Mark sat in his car, staring at the dashboard as the motor quietly hummed. At 7:30 a.m., he was exhausted. His mind was preoccupied with deadlines, meetings, and an endless to-do list that felt impossible to finish. He'd been working 12-hour days for months, skipping lunch and foregoing weekends to keep up. But rather than moving forward, he felt as if he was sinking deeper.

Mark wasn't always like this. A year ago, he was pleased with his job. He was committed to his job and took pride in being the go-to person for his team. But then the spark was gone. What had once empowered him was now completely depleting him. His stress levels were high, and he felt disconnected from his job, family, and himself. The weight of it all was overwhelming, and the thought of going another day in this state of exhaustion made him physically ill.

As the weeks went on, Mark detected signs that something was seriously wrong. He was upset with his coworkers, erupting over little arguments. His sleep was erratic, and he struggled to focus on even small tasks. More worrying, he began to wonder if he was still qualified for his job. The sense of achievement that had once pushed him had vanished, replaced by a hollow emptiness that made him wonder whether all his efforts had been for naught.

Mark was suffering from burnout, a condition marked by emotional, mental, and physical exhaustion as a result of persistent stress. However, like many others, he did not understand it until he was well into the cycle.

Understanding Burnout

Burnout is more than simply being weary or stressed out. It's a chronic condition that develops over time when we are subjected to constant demands with insufficient opportunity to relax, recoup, or recharge. It's the feeling that no matter how hard you work, it will never be enough. Burnout causes you to lose your sense of accomplishment and motivation, and it can sometimes lead to you questioning your self-worth and identity.

Burnout impacts people from many professions and areas of life. Whether you're a corporate executive, a teacher, a healthcare worker, or a stay-at-home mom, anyone can experience burnout if they push themselves too hard for too long. Recognizing the signs of burnout early on and taking purposeful actions to prioritize self-care and balance are critical to overcoming it.

There are three primary dimensions of burnout:

1. Emotional Exhaustion: The feeling of being emotionally exhausted and depleted of all vigor, often to the point that you fear you have nothing more to give. Emotional exhaustion can lead to cynicism, irritability, and disengagement from work or other obligations.

2. Depersonalization or Cynicism: This is the emotional separation from your work or those around you. You may become numb or indifferent to tasks you formerly enjoyed, or you may develop a negative, cynical attitude toward your career or coworkers.

3. Reduced Personal Achievement: Burnout typically results in feelings of ineffectiveness and failure. You may begin to believe that your efforts are futile and that you are not making a substantial difference, thus undermining your motivation and self-esteem.

Signs of Burnout

Many people's burnout symptoms begin mildly. The symptoms may begin with weariness or frustration, but they intensify over time. Here are some common signs of burnout to look out for:

- Chronic Fatigue: Feeling tired all the time, even after a full night's sleep.

- Difficulty Concentrating: Struggling to focus on tasks or make decisions.

- Loss of Interest: Feeling disconnected from activities or projects you once enjoyed.

- Irritability: Becoming easily frustrated or short-tempered with others.

- Physical Symptoms: Experiencing headaches, muscle tension, or stomach issues as a result of stress.

- Feeling Overwhelmed: Feeling like you're drowning in responsibilities and can't keep up.

Mark's tale is a textbook case of burnout. He began with excitement, but as the demands of his job grew, he pushed himself more, rarely taking moments to relax or recover. His emotional and physical tiredness worsened, and he could no longer enjoy the job he once enjoyed.

How to manage burnout.

If you relate to Mark's tale, you're not alone. Burnout is rather frequent, but the good news is that it can be avoided and managed. Here are some ways to combat burnout and regain your feeling of balance:

1. Establish Boundaries: Learning to draw proper lines between work and personal life is one of the most critical stages toward avoiding burnout. This could mean saying no to extra chores, restricting after-hours emails, or setting aside time for yourself free of work obligations. Boundaries help to create the necessary space for rest and recharging.

2. Prioritize Self-Care: When we feel overburdened, we frequently neglect self-care, which is critical to our mental and physical health. Small acts of self-care, such as taking breaks during the day, going for a walk, practicing mindfulness, or simply getting adequate sleep, can all help to prevent burnout.

3. Delegate and Ask for Help: You do not have to do everything yourself. If your workload becomes unmanageable, delegate tasks to others or seek assistance from a supervisor or colleague. Learning to share responsibilities can help you minimize stress and prevent burnout.

4. Take breaks: Regular breaks throughout the day are vital for maintaining focus and energy. Take a break from your desk, go for a walk, or spend some time practicing deep breathing. These breaks will reset your brain and allow you to refuel.

5. Reassess Your Priorities: Burnout typically occurs when we aim for unrealistic goals or place too much pressure on ourselves. Take a step back and consider your priorities. What tasks are truly critical, and what could be eliminated? By focusing on what is most important, you can reduce stress and make the process more achievable.

6. Reconnect with Your Purpose: One of the most devastating repercussions of burnout is a loss of meaning in your work. Take a moment to contemplate why you began your work or role in the first place. What aroused your curiosity first? What kind of influence do you hope to have? Reconnecting with your mission can reignite your passion and help you persist through difficult circumstances.

Mark's Turning Point

Mark understood that continuing on the same path would have serious consequences for his health and well-being. After seeing a counselor, he realized he had been ignoring his own needs in favor of constantly pushing for more. His counselor helped him build a burnout prevention approach that includes taking frequent breaks, setting boundaries, and learning how to delegate tasks at work.

Mark eventually regained his sense of self. He no longer dreaded going to work, and his excitement for the job gradually returned. Most importantly, he recognized that caring for himself was not a sign of weakness, but rather a necessary step toward becoming his best self in both his professional and personal life.

Moving Forward

Burnout is a serious condition that anyone can get, but it does not have to be permanent. Burnout can be combated and prevented from taking over your life by taking proactive steps to care for your emotional and physical health, setting boundaries, and prioritizing what is truly important. Remember that your productivity does not define you, and adequate relaxation is essential for long-term success and well-being.

12

Managing Work-Related Stress

"Work is important, but your well-being is essential. Learn to set boundaries, manage your time, and prioritize your mental health—because no job is worth sacrificing your peace of mind."

Relatable Story

Samantha sat at her desk, her heart beating as she watched the cursor blink on her computer screen. She had a huge presentation due at the end of the week, two meetings today, and over a hundred unread emails in her inbox. The weight of her responsibilities pressed down on her like a heavy blanket, sapping her energy and excitement. As she sipped her third cup of coffee, she realized that caffeine alone was insufficient to alleviate the stress that had been building inside her for weeks.

Samantha wasn't alone. Many people are overwhelmed by work-related stress, especially in today's fast-paced, always-on atmosphere. Every time her phone vibrated with another email or notice, her stress level increased. She felt trapped in an endless cycle of activities and expectations, with no time to catch her breath. The pressure to perform well, meet deadlines, and exceed expectations weighed hard on her, negatively impacting not only her professional life but also her mental health and relationships.

Samantha was tired when she arrived home at the end of the day. Instead of sleeping or spending time with her family, she found herself lying in bed, eagerly checking emails and preparing her day. Sleep became elusive, and tension permeated every aspect of her life.

Understanding Work-Related Stress

Work-related stress is one of the most common mental health concerns that people face. Stress in the workplace, whether induced by pressure to meet deadlines, deal with difficult coworkers, or balance a heavy workload, may have a significant impact on both physical and mental well-being. Unlike a brief period of pressure, which can sometimes encourage us, chronic stress builds up over time and can become overwhelming, leading to burnout, anxiety, and even depression.

When stress becomes severe, it affects more than just our professional performance. It seeps into our personal lives, influencing our relationships, sleeping patterns, and even our physical health. Many people, including Samantha, struggle to leave employment. With technological advancements and remote working, the boundaries between professional and personal life have blurred, making it more difficult to unplug and rejuvenate.

Symptoms of work-related stress

Before we begin managing stress, it's critical to recognize the signs that work-related stress is taking over:

1. Irritability: Minor inconveniences become major irritants, and you find yourself snapping at coworkers or family members.

2. Fatigue: Despite getting enough sleep, you're constantly fatigued and unable to concentrate or engage in your tasks.

3. Physical Symptoms: Stress can cause headaches, muscle stiffness, digestive issues, and even high blood pressure.

4. Reduced Performance: Once manageable Tasks now appear intimidating, and your productivity begins to decline.

5. Insomnia: Stress often results in restless evenings, making it difficult to fall and stay asleep.

6. Withdrawal: You may start to shun social events or overlook personal ties because you are too focused on work or too tired to participate.

Samantha had nearly all of these symptoms, but like many others, dismissed them as "just part of the job." She vowed herself she would push through, but ignoring the signs of stress just made things worse.

Effects of Chronic Stress

Chronic work-related stress, if not managed appropriately, can result in serious mental health problems such as anxiety disorders, depression, and burnout. It also increases the risk of physical health problems such as heart disease, low immune function, and gastrointestinal diseases.

Samantha's health declined as a result of the constant stress she was experiencing. She began experiencing migraines and digestive problems, which she initially dismissed as usual signs of a demanding lifestyle. When her doctor asked about her stress levels during a routine check-up, Samantha felt her body was sending her a clear message: something needed to change.

How to Manage Work-Related Stress

Fortunately, there are effective techniques to manage and reduce work-related stress. The idea is to identify when stress becomes unbearable and take proactive steps to address it. Here are some strategies to consider.

1. Time Management: Efficient time management is one of the most effective stress-reduction strategies. Divide your projects into reasonable chunks, establish realistic deadlines, and prioritize your work by importance. Calendars, to-do lists, and project management software can all help you keep organized.

   - The 90-Minute Rule: Divide your day into 90-minute intervals. Work for 90 minutes, then take a 10-15 minute break to rest and refuel. This pattern corresponds to your body's natural energy cycles, allowing you to remain focused and avoid exhaustion.

2. Learn to Say No: One of the most common causes of stress in the office is taking on more than you can handle. Set boundaries by denying initiatives or tasks that you know will overwhelm you. It's better to accomplish fewer things well than overwork and underperform.

3. Mindfulness and Relaxation Techniques: Including mindfulness activities like meditation or deep breathing exercises in your daily routine will help you stay grounded and minimize stress. Even a few minutes spent focusing on your breath will help you relax and cleanse your mind.

4. Exercise and Physical Activity: Physical activity is one of the most effective ways to reduce stress. Exercise, whether it's a quick walk during your lunch break, a yoga session, or a workout after work, releases endorphins, which make you feel better and reduces anxiety.

5. Talk to Someone: If you're feeling overwhelmed, don't be hesitant to seek help. Discussing your stress with a coworker, manager, or mental health professional might help you obtain new perspectives and suggestions. Samantha noticed that simply talking to a trusted friend about her work stress made her feel lighter and less alone in her struggles.

6. Set Work-Life Boundaries: In today's digital world, work can easily intrude on personal time. Set clear limits by assigning specific work hours and adhering to them. For example, disable email notifications after a certain period, or create a separate workspace at home so that when you leave, you mentally check out of work.

7. Take Breaks and Vacations: It's easy to fall into the trap of thinking that you have to work constantly to succeed. However, regular breaks and holidays are required for both mental and physical wellness. Taking time away from work allows you to recharge and return with a fresh perspective.

Samantha's Turning Point

Samantha started minimizing her work-related stress with little improvement. She began by scheduling small breaks throughout the day and limiting her work hours. Rather than staying up late to finish emails, she made a point of not reading work emails after 7 p.m. She also started taking yoga classes twice a week to help her relax.

Most importantly, Samantha asked her supervisor for assistance. She acknowledged feeling stressed and asked for help in prioritizing her responsibilities. To her surprise, her supervisor understood and worked with her to shift some tasks, making her job more bearable.

Samantha felt better in control of her tension after a few weeks. She still had a full schedule, but she no longer felt like she was drowning. She restored her sense of well-being and equilibrium after taking proactive steps to control her stress.

Moving Forward:

While work-related stress is unavoidable, it does not have to take over your life. You can have a happier, more balanced work-life by detecting stress symptoms early on and taking action to control them. Remember that it is acceptable to seek help, establish boundaries, and prioritize your mental health. After all, you can't perform well if you're continuously running low on energy.

13:

Facing Financial Anxiety

"Financial anxiety thrives in silence and fear. By facing your financial challenges head-on and seeking support, you can regain control over your money—and your peace of mind."

Relatable Story

James sat in his small apartment, staring at a stack of outstanding bills on the kitchen table. The rent was due, his car needed maintenance, and he had recently received an unexpected medical bill. As the weight of these financial obligations pressed down on him, his chest tightened. He had always been frugal with money, but despite his best efforts, it appeared that he would never succeed.

Financial worries had been a regular companion in James' life, but they had gotten worse during the last year. A wage cut at work due to financial constraints had worsened his mounting stress. He found himself constantly calculating how much money he still had in his bank account, fretting over every penny spent, and losing sleep over what the future might hold. His anxiousness made it difficult for him to concentrate at work, and his social life suffered as he avoided going out with friends to save money.

Millions of people have had similar experiences to James'. In today's world, financial stress is a key source of anxiety. Whether it's due to job uncertainty, debt, or unexpected expenses, the fear of not having enough money can leave you feeling overwhelmed, helpless, and alone.

Understanding Financial Anxiety

Financial anxiety is the fear or stress generated by financial concerns. It can manifest in a variety of ways, ranging from concern about paying bills on time to dread of losing a job. It's more than just not having enough money; it's the persistent fear that something may go wrong financially, leaving you worse off than before.

In James' case, his financial anxiety arose from several factors. Despite having a solid job, the sudden pay cut had him apprehensive about his future. The rising expense of living, along with unexpected bills, increased his concerns. He felt like he was constantly walking a tightrope, frightened that one wrong move might send his financial world crashing down.

Signs of Financial Anxiety

Many people experience financial anxiety without realizing the impact on their emotional and physical well-being. Here are some frequent indicators:

1. Constant Worry: You are always anxious about your financial situation, even though you have little control over it.

2. Avoidance: You avoid opening bills, checking your bank account, or dealing with financial problems because they are too difficult to face.

3. Physical Symptoms: Anxiety can result in headaches, tiredness, insomnia, and even digestive issues.

4. Isolation: You avoid social activities and interactions because you are afraid of wasting money or being judged for your financial situation.

5. Panic Attacks: In extreme cases, financial stress can trigger panic attacks, making it impossible to breathe, think straight, or handle overwhelming anxiety.

James' anxiousness began to impair every aspect of his life. He stopped going out with friends, not only to conserve money but also because the prospect of spending money made him nervous. He'd lie awake at night, mentally calculating his bills and unable to find a solution. There seemed to be no way out, and the stress was increasing.

Impact of Financial Anxiety

Financial issues can have a huge negative impact on an individual. It has an impact on mental health, resulting in increased anxiety, despair, and stress. Persistent worry can wear a person down over time, leading to burnout and other serious mental health problems.

Financial anxiety erodes connections. Partners may disagree over money, and individuals may withdraw from family or friends because they are too ashamed or stressed to discuss financial issues. It can also influence job performance because chronic worry makes it difficult to concentrate or stay motivated.

In James' situation, his uneasiness began to affect his performance at work. He became preoccupied during meetings, constantly worrying about how he would make his next set of payments. His manager saw his lack of focus and production, which increased his stress as he feared losing his job.

How to Overcome Financial Anxiety

While financial anxiety is common, there are strategies to manage it effectively and regain control over your financial well-being. The key is to take practical steps that help reduce the uncertainty and stress associated with financial issues.

1. Make a Budget: One of the most effective strategies to relieve financial stress is to develop a realistic budget. A budget provides a clear picture of your income, expenses, and savings. Tracking where your money goes allows you to find areas where you may decrease costs and shift funds to essential financial goals like debt repayment or emergency savings.

--Begin small. James started by tracking his everyday expenses. He downloaded a budgeting tool that allowed him to easily track every purchase and spending. Seeing his expenses written down in front of him helped him find areas where he could save money, such as dining out or subscription services that he no longer needed.

2. Establish an Emergency Fund: The fear of unanticipated bills is a common source of financial stress. An emergency fund can help alleviate this burden. Begin by depositing a small percentage of each paycheck into a savings account. Even if you only save a small amount at a time, it will accumulate over time and serve as a safety net in the event of an emergency.

- James' Fund: James set a goal to save $50 from each paycheck. It wasn't much, but it signaled the start. His emergency fund expanded over time, and knowing he had something to fall back on helped him feel less concerned.

3. Address Debt Step by Step: Debt is one of the most common causes of financial stress. If you're suffering from debt, break it down into manageable bits. Pay off high-interest debt first, then consider consolidating your obligations or consulting with a financial advisor about a repayment strategy.

- Debt Snowball: James had a lot of credit card debt. He used the debt snowball technique, paying off his smallest debt first, then progressing to the next, generating momentum with each paid-off bill.

4. Seek Professional Help: If your financial situation is overwhelming, do not be hesitant to seek help. Financial advisers, credit counselors, and even mental health professionals can assist you in managing your finances and the stress associated with it.

5. Practice Mindfulness and Stress Management: Dealing with financial concerns is about more than just money; it's also about taking care of your mental health. When financial stress begins to overwhelm you, employ mindfulness techniques such as meditation or deep breathing to help you relax. Exercise and physical activity are also effective ways to reduce stress and improve your mood.

- James' Routine: To calm his nerves, James began going for a walk every evening. It allowed him to clear his mind and let go of the anxiousness he'd been experiencing throughout the day.

6. Talk About It: Money is sometimes a taboo subject, yet keeping your financial concerns to yourself might make matters worse. Inform a trusted friend, partner, or financial advisor about your concerns. Sharing your

burden can make it feel lighter and bring new perspectives on how to tackle your financial problems.

- James' Support: James told his sister about his financial problems. To his astonishment, she had been in a similar circumstance and had given him advice on how she handled her financial anxiety.

Moving forward.

Financial stress may appear insurmountable, but by taking modest, attainable measures, you can recover control over your financial and mental health. Building a budget, setting up an emergency fund, and reducing debt one step at a time can all help to alleviate the uncertainties associated with financial stress.

James' path was not simple, but by proactive efforts, he gradually achieved control of his finances. His fear did not go away instantly, but it became more manageable, and he began to see a path forward.

14

Coping with Chronic Illness

"Chronic illness may change the way you live, but it doesn't have to take away your ability to find joy, purpose, and peace in the present moment."

Sarah sat calmly in the doctor's office, her heart pounding as she waited for the results. She'd been suffering from unexplained tiredness, joint discomfort, and other chronic symptoms for months, interfering with her normal activities. She had gone from being active and engaged in her career and social life to fighting to get out of bed in the morning. When the doctor finally spoke, it hit Sarah like a punch in the gut: she had a chronic autoimmune condition.

On one occasion, her life changed. Managing this disease would become a regular part of her routine. The overpowering sense of ambiguity weighed on her. How would she maintain her work, care for her family, and find joy in life while in constant pain and fatigue? The mental and emotional toll seemed almost as daunting as the physical challenges.

Sarah's story resonates with millions of people worldwide who suffer from chronic illnesses. Chronic illness can lead to significant loss—not only in physical ability, but also in one's sense of self, autonomy, and purpose. It typically involves a considerable change in our approach to life, work, and relationships.

Understanding Chronic Illness

Chronic illnesses are long-term conditions that can be managed but not cured. The conditions include diabetes, autoimmune disorders, heart disease, chronic fatigue syndrome, and fibromyalgia. Coping with a chronic illness usually entails creating techniques to adjust to the constraints it imposes while preserving as much control over your life as possible.

For Sarah, this was learning to pace herself and listen to her body. She no longer had the freedom to work late into the night or go on spontaneous trips with friends. She had to carefully organize her activities, get enough rest, and manage her symptoms with medication and lifestyle changes.

The Emotional and Psychological Toll

Being diagnosed with a chronic illness can elicit a range of emotions. Shock, denial, rage, sadness, and even guilt are common responses. There is occasionally a period of grief for the life you once had, and many people are overwhelmed by the unknown of what comes next.

Sarah went on an emotional rollercoaster after learning of her diagnosis. She originally couldn't believe it. She had always been healthy, so why now? She was outraged with her body for betraying her, followed by guilt. She felt as if she was failing her family and colleagues, incapable of being the person she previously was.

These emotional issues add to the burden of living with a chronic illness. Physical symptoms must be handled, but so must the mental and emotional burdens that accompany them.

Common Challenges of Living with Chronic Illness

1. Tiredness and Pain: Many chronic diseases induce constant tiredness and pain, making even simple chores appear daunting. This constant state of physical discomfort can wear on your mental resilience, making it difficult to be happy.

2. Uncertainty: Chronic illness is generally unpredictable. Symptoms can come unexpectedly, leaving you feeling as if you never have full control over your body or routine.

3. Social Isolation: Many persons with chronic illnesses avoid social gatherings because they can't keep up or feel misunderstood. Friends may not fully appreciate the limitations of the disease, leading to feelings of loneliness.

4. Identity Crisis: Chronic sickness can drastically alter how you see yourself. If you used to take pride in being active and self-sufficient, adjusting to a life where you need more help and have physical limitations may be tough to accept.

5. Mental Health Issues: Those with chronic illnesses are more likely to experience depression and anxiety. The constant stress of managing symptoms, doctor appointments, and prescriptions can be detrimental to your mental health.

How to deal with chronic illnesses.

Living with a chronic illness can be stressful, but there are some strategies and mindsets that can make it easier. The goal is to prioritize both physical and mental health, creating a balance that allows you to adjust while maintaining your sense of enjoyment and meaning in life.

1. Pacing and Planning: Learning to pace oneself is one of the most important skills for managing a chronic condition. Accept that your energy and abilities may fluctuate from day to day. You can reduce your risk of burnout or flare-ups by planning your activities and taking breaks as needed.

- Sarah's Strategy: Sarah created a timetable to accommodate her energy levels throughout the day. She emphasized the most important tasks in the mornings, when she had more energy, and saved the afternoons for relaxation or less difficult activities.

2. Mindfulness and Acceptance: Chronic illness often needs a change in attitude. Mindfulness—being present at the moment—can help ease the mental strain caused by worrying about the future or dwelling on the past. Acceptance does not indicate giving up; rather, it entails acknowledging your limitations and working within them without letting them define you.

- Finding Peace: Sarah started meditating, which helped her focus on the present moment rather than worrying about her illness. Mindfulness exercises helped her handle her stress and anxiety more effectively.

3. Creating a Support System: Chronic disease can be lonely, but you do not have to face it alone. Interacting with individuals who understand your situation, whether through friends, family, or support organizations, can bring you emotional comfort. Talking to a therapist who specializes in chronic diseases might also help you process your emotions.

- Support Networks: Sarah found an online support group for people with her disease. Hearing other people's tales and expressing her own made her feel less alienated and more optimistic.

4. Focus on What You Can Manage: While chronic illness can make life feel uncertain, focusing on what you can control can bring a sense of empowerment. This could entail managing your treatment plan, changing your lifestyle, or setting small, manageable goals to help you feel accomplished.

- Small Wins: Rather than focusing on everything she could no longer accomplish, Sarah began setting small daily goals such as going for a short walk or completing a hobby project. Celebrating these tiny accomplishments gave her a sense of control over her life.

5. Educate Yourself: Understanding your condition is critical for managing it well. Discover your ailment, treatment options, and lifestyle changes that can improve your quality of life. The more informed you are, the more equipped you will be to advocate for yourself in medical situations.

6. Prioritize emotional health: Because chronic illness is a long-term battle, taking care of your emotional health is just as important as managing your physical symptoms. Counseling, therapy, or simply journaling can help you process your emotions and develop coping mechanisms during difficult times.

   - Therapy as a Tool: Sarah began working with a therapist to help her cope with her grief and loss. In addition, the therapist taught her cognitive-behavioral methods for dealing with negative thought patterns.

Living Well with Chronic Illness

Living with a chronic illness may require you to reevaluate your approach to life, but it does not preclude you from living a full life. By focusing on what you can control, building a strong support network, and prioritizing your mental and physical health, you can overcome the challenges of chronic disease while still enjoying everyday life.

Sarah took some time to get used to her new normal. She learned to pace herself, accept support from loved ones, and find new activities that suited her energy level. Her chronic illness did not go away, but her life became more manageable—and even meaningful—when she chose to concentrate on what she could do rather than what she couldn't.

15

Healing from Relationship Breakdowns

"Heartbreak may shatter us, but in picking up the pieces, we find the strength to rebuild, learning that healing begins with self-love and forgiveness."

Relatable Story

Rachel stared blankly at the ceiling, her heart heavy from their separation. After five years with someone she thought was "the one," her relationship ended in a swirl of confusion, hurt, and rage. She was grieving not only the death of a spouse but also the loss of the future she had imagined. Everything they had planned together—moving in, traveling, and creating a family—was suddenly gone.

She spent the next two weeks in a trance, replaying every conversation and quarrel in her thoughts, wondering what went wrong. The breakup had a profound emotional impact on her, influencing every element of her life. She struggled to concentrate at work, withdrew herself from her friends, and felt as if she was carrying a hidden wound that no one could see.

Rachel's story is one that many of us can relate to. Relationship breakdowns are typically among the most difficult emotional experiences a person can endure. The sense of loss may be terrible, whether it's the end of a sexual relationship, a friendship, or even a familial split.

Understanding Relationship Breakdowns

Miscommunication, unfulfilled expectations, betrayal, or simply growing apart are some of the reasons partnerships might end. Regardless of the cause, the emotional aftermath can leave us saddened, questioning our self-worth, and confused about how to move forward.

Rachel's separation was caused by a gradual shift in priorities and goals. She and her lover had grown apart over time, with different desires. What began as minor arguments about plans became into major issues that neither could resolve. The revelation that the person she loved no longer aligned with her life's objectives was tough but necessary.

The Emotional Stages of Healing

Healing from a relationship breakdown often mirrors the stages of grief, and each person moves through them at their own pace.

1. Denial: At first, it is difficult to recognize that the relationship is truly over. There is a sense of incredulity, and many people remain hopeful that things will be resolved. Rachel spent weeks thinking about all of the "what ifs"—what if she had said something different, what if they had tried harder, what if they had simply taken a break instead of calling it quits?

2. Anger: As the reality of the split sinks in, you may become angry. This can be fury aimed against another person, oneself, or the situation as a whole. Rachel was upset with her ex-partner for not putting more effort into the relationship, as well as with herself for not detecting the warning signs earlier.

3. Bargaining: Many people try to "bargain" their way out of a breakup. This could entail reaching out to the other person in the hopes of rekindling the relationship or making promises to oneself about how they will change. Rachel attempted to reach out several times. Thinking

that maybe they could talk through their issues, but each conversation only made her feel more hopeless.

4. Depression: Once the anger and bargaining have passed, many people experience sadness and withdrawal. This is the point at which the full weight of the loss becomes obvious, and it may be difficult to find inspiration or joy in daily life. Rachel felt as if she were sinking into a void, and getting out of bed seemed impossible.

5. Acceptance: Finally, with patience and self-care, acceptance is achieved. This does not mean that the person's pain is over, but it does suggest that they are ready to move on, accepting the loss of the relationship and focusing on rebuilding their lives. Rachel eventually reached a place where she could reflect on the relationship without becoming obsessed with it. She recognized that, while the separation was tough, both she and her ex-partner needed to evolve.

Common Challenges After a Breakup

1. Identity Loss: Following a long-term relationship, your identity may become inextricably linked with the other person. Following a breakup, many people struggle to restore their identity outside of the romantic relationship. Rachel, who had based much of her future on her lover, was disoriented following their breakup, unsure who she was without him.

2. Loneliness: The loss of a relationship often results in significant feelings of loneliness. Daily interactions, support, and companionship are abruptly removed, leaving a gap that can become overwhelming at times.

3. Self-Doubt: After a breakup, it's natural to question your worth and worry if you'll ever find love again. Rachel found herself wondering if she was enough—whether she was lovable, worthy, or had failed in some way.

4. Fear of the Future: The unknowns of the future might be frightening. When a relationship ends, the goals and ambitions you had for the future vanish, leaving you with a blank slate that may be both liberating and terrifying.

Steps to Healing After a Relationship Breakdown

Healing from a relationship breakup is a process, and while time is vital, you can take proactive steps to help yourself move forward.

1. Allow Yourself to Grieve: It is vital to recognize your pain and allow yourself to feel it. Suppressing your emotions can only slow the healing process. Cry if necessary, write down your feelings, or talk to someone you trust.

   - Rachel's Grief: Rachel allowed herself to feel the full spectrum of her emotions. Instead of pretending everything was well, she allowed herself to grieve, writing down her thoughts and speaking with close friends.

2. Rediscover Yourself: Use this time to reconnect with who you are outside of your relationship. Explore hobbies, passions, and interests that you may have put on hold throughout your relationship.

   - Rachel's Self-Rediscovery: Rachel enrolled in a local art class, something she had always wanted to take but never had time for. It became a way for her to express herself and rediscover her sense of self.

3. Seek Help: During this time, talk to your friends, family, or a therapist. Talking about your emotions can help you deal with your pain and gain perspective.

- Getting Help: Rachel started seeing a therapist who specialized in relationship counseling. This provided her with a safe space to address her feelings of loss and confusion.

4. Prioritize self-care: Take care of your physical, emotional, and mental health. Exercise, meditation, or spending time outside are all things that can help you relax and enjoy yourself.

- Rachel's Self-Care Routine: She began practicing yoga, which has helped her both physically and mentally. The mindfulness aspect of yoga helped her stay grounded during stressful moments.

5. Set Boundaries: If you find yourself constantly checking your ex's social media or attempting to stay in touch, it's critical to establish boundaries. Distance could help you heal and gain understanding.

- Setting Boundaries: Rachel made the difficult decision to unfollow her ex on social media after realizing that seeing his posts was keeping her from moving on.

6. Allow Yourself to Hope: Even if it seems impossible in the aftermath of a breakup, believe that happiness and love will find you again. Healing from a failed relationship does not imply that you will never love again; rather, it indicates that you are prepared for something far better.

Living Beyond the Heartbreak

Healing after a relationship breakdown is a non-linear process. There will be days when you feel like you're making progress and days when the pain is as fresh as the day it ended. However, with time, self-care, and support, you will grow stronger, wiser, and more aware of your own needs and goals.

Rachel's breakup represented a turning point in her life. Despite the suffering, it helped her reconnect with herself and reconfirm her life and relationship goals. She realized that her worth was independent of another person and that she could still love herself and others.

16

Embracing Change and Uncertainty

"Change may be unsettling, but it is in the unknown that we grow. Embracing uncertainty allows us to discover new possibilities and the resilience within ourselves."

Relatable Story

isha has always excelled in routines. She appreciated knowing what would come next—the regularity of her daily routine, the familiarity of her job, and the comfort of her relationships. But all changed when the employer she had been with for ten years announced that they were downsizing. Her position, like many others, was being eliminated.

The news hit her like a tidal wave. For weeks after the announcement, Aisha struggled to comprehend the rapid change. She felt like the rug had been pulled from under her feet, and the ground underneath her rocked. What should she do right now? How would she pay her bills? And, more importantly, who was she if not the experienced professional she had been for the previous decade?

Change, particularly when imposed upon us, maybe terrifying. Aisha's story is one of many involving life-changing events, such as job loss, relationship breakdown, migration to a new place, or a significant health crisis. The uncertainty associated with such a shift may leave us feeling adrift, frightened, and afraid.

Understanding Change and Uncertainty

Change is unavoidable. Life is full of surprises, whether we are prepared for them or not. Regardless of how often we experience change, it can still feel like an upheaval. Uncertainty often accompanies change, leaving us with more questions than answers. Change can be difficult because we are wired to seek stability and predictability.

Aisha's struggle with uncertainty after losing her job is something we can all relate to. The future she had once been so secure in was now full of unknowns. Her experience teaches us that, while change is an unavoidable aspect of life, how we respond to it often dictates how we proceed.

Why We Fear Change

Fear of change and uncertainty can arise from a variety of sources:

1. Loss of Control: Change might make us feel like we've lost control of our own lives. When circumstances change unexpectedly, we frequently rush to recover a sense of stability. Aisha thought that losing her work meant losing control of her future. She had a clear professional plan, but it was now gone.

2. Fear of the Unknown: People seek certainty and comfort in knowing what they may expect. When faced with ambiguity, we tend to contemplate the worst-case scenario. Aisha became worried: what if she couldn't find another job? What happens if her savings run out?

3. Attachment to the Past: We frequently resist change because we are attached to the way things were. It might be difficult to let go of what is comfortable, even if it no longer benefits us. Aisha was very tied to her professional identity at her employer, and letting it go seemed like a loss.

4. Fear of Failure: Change typically brings new issues, and with them comes the fear of failing in unfamiliar territory. Aisha was scared she would be unable to adjust to a new profession or career, therefore she resisted taking advantage of the chances that awaited her.

The Importance of Embracing Change

While fear of change is understandable, it is also important to remember that change frequently leads to growth, new opportunities, and the chance of reinvention. Accepting change allows us to adapt, evolve, and eventually thrive in new environments.

Aisha's watershed moment came when she understood that, while she couldn't change the fact that her job was gone, she could control how she handled the circumstance. Instead of focusing on the uncertainty, she saw the change as an opportunity to explore other career avenues that she had not previously considered.

How to Embrace Change and Uncertainty

Here are some practical techniques to help you accept change and overcome uncertainty:

1. Acknowledge your feelings. It is normal to feel fearful, apprehensive, or frustrated in the face of change. Don't try to suppress your emotions. Recognize them, but do not allow emotions to influence your behavior. Allow yourself to experience feelings, but realize that they will pass.

- Aisha's acceptance: She allowed herself to regret the loss of her job. She reflected on her worries and doubts, but she did not let them immobilize her.

2. Change Your Perspective: Rather than viewing change as something to fear, consider it a chance for progress. Change frequently takes us outside of our comfort zones, where true growth occurs.

- Reframing the Situation: Aisha saw her job loss as a chance to rediscover her passions. She realized that the job she had previously enjoyed had become monotonous and that this shift could provide the incentive she needed to pursue something more fulfilling.

3. Concentrate on What You Can Control: While you may be unable to change the situation, you can influence how you react to it. Instead of being paralyzed by fear of the unknown, focus on the steps you can take to go forward.

- Taking Action: Aisha started updating her resume, networking with old coworkers, and looking for new professional prospects. She took back control of the situation by focusing on her strengths.

4. Practice Mindfulness and Patience: While change and uncertainty can be stressful, practicing mindfulness can help you stay present in the moment. Take one step at a time and be gentle with yourself while you make the transition.

- Aisha's Mindfulness Practice: To alleviate her anxiety, Aisha started practicing meditation and journaling every morning. This enabled her to remain grounded and calm in the face of uncertainty.

141

5. Seek Support: You do not have to go through change alone. Contact friends, family, or a mentor for assistance. Talking to someone who has experienced a similar scenario may provide insight and comfort.

- Seeking Support: Aisha told her close friends about her doubts and concerns. Their encouragement and advice made her feel less alone and more confident in her ability to make the transition.

6. Value Flexibility: Being adaptive is one of the most effective ways to navigate change. Life rarely goes as planned, but being adaptable allows you to handle the unexpected graciously.

  - Adapting to Change: Aisha was first resistant to the idea of changing work lines, but as she researched new industries, she became excited about the possibilities. Her drive to be adaptable opened up alternatives that she had not considered before.

Living with Uncertainty

While change can bring both growth and new opportunities, uncertainty can be difficult to handle. The trick is to learn to handle uncertainty without being overwhelmed. Accept that the future is uncertain and, rather than striving to predict it, focus on making the most of the present moment.

Aisha had no idea what her next career would be, but instead of letting the uncertainty overwhelm her, she chose to focus on what she could do each day to move forward. She applied for jobs, took online courses to better her skills, and remained open to whatever came next. Over time, the uncertainty subsided, and she realized she was capable of dealing with whatever the future contained.

Thriving Through Change

Accepting change and learning to live with uncertainty might help you become more resilient and flexible. Life will always throw you curveballs, but how you deal with them will shape your future.

Aisha eventually found a job in a different field, which not only reignited her excitement but also gave her more work-life balance. Looking back, she realized that, while losing her previous job was difficult, it acted as a catalyst for positive change in her life.

Embracing change does not erase fear, but it does mean that you move forward despite it, realizing that uncertainty is a part of life and that each step you take makes you stronger.

17

Developing Emotional Intelligence

"Emotional intelligence is not about being less emotional; it's about being more aware of your emotions and using them to build stronger connections and make better decisions."

Relatable Story

Meet Carlos. He was a manager at a medium-sized technology company and was well-known for his intelligence, work ethic, and ability to meet deadlines. On paper, he seemed like the ideal employee. However, Carlos had a recurring issue: his connections with coworkers were strained, and his team frequently felt estranged from him. Carlos was technically skilled, but he lacked emotional intelligence, which cannot be measured solely via production.

Carlos recalls a breakthrough moment. During a team meeting, there was some disagreement over the project's direction. Carlos convinced that his approach was superior, ignored his team's worries without listening. As tensions rose, one of his most faithful employees stormed out of the meeting, dissatisfied and outraged. The fallout was fast. Several team members left the project, and morale deteriorated.

For the first time, Carlos realized that, no matter how great he was at his job, he lacked one critical skill: the ability to understand and control not only his own emotions but also those of his coworkers. This discovery prompted Carlos to go on a journey to increase his emotional intelligence, a decision that had far-reaching implications for both his professional and personal relationships. Understanding Emotional Intelligence (EI)

Emotional intelligence, also known as EI or EQ (Emotional Quotient), is the ability to recognize, evaluate, and control one's own emotions while simultaneously perceiving and influencing the emotions of others. Unlike IQ, which tests cognitive capacity, emotional intelligence assesses interpersonal dynamics and emotional sensitivity.

Carlos' high IQ allowed him to thrive at problem-solving and decision-making, but his low emotional intelligence hampered his ability to collaborate, communicate effectively, and sympathize with his team members. EI is frequently seen as a critical component of personal and professional success because it enables us to build stronger bonds, make more informed decisions, and manage more effectively with stress.

Components of Emotional Intelligence

Emotional intelligence is usually separated into four main components:

1. Self-awareness: The ability to recognize and understand one's own emotions, as well as how they influence one's thoughts and actions. It all boils down to understanding your abilities and flaws, as well as having self-esteem.

   - Carlos' Self-awareness: Before the incident with his coworkers, Carlos had rarely considered how his emotions affected his interpersonal relationships. He was unaware that his rage and impatience during meetings were causing conflict among his team members. Becoming self-aware was the first step toward improving his emotional intelligence.

2. Self-Management: The ability to control impulsive thoughts and behaviors, healthily manage emotions, take initiative, and maintain promises. This includes keeping emotional control and staying cool in difficult times.

146

- Carlos' Self-Management: Carlos had always prided himself on his ability to remain calm under pressure, but he soon discovered that he was typically repressing his emotions rather than managing them. When conflict erupted during his team meetings, it was because he had not addressed the underlying issues.

3. Social Awareness: The ability to understand other people's emotions, desires, and worries, recognize emotional clues, and feel at ease in social situations. This necessitates empathy, which is the ability to see things from the perspective of another.

- Carlos's Social Awareness: Carlos' lack of empathy was one of his most critical issues. He frequently focused completely on the task at hand, ignoring his coworkers' emotional states. As his social awareness grew, he learned to listen to his coworkers' feelings and respond sympathetically.

4. Relationship Management: The capacity to form and maintain strong bonds, communicate effectively, inspire and influence others, work well in groups, and handle conflict.

- Carlos' Relationship Management: After committing to actively working on his emotional intelligence, Carlos saw a difference in his approach toward relationships. Instead of reacting defensively to criticism, he began having open and helpful interactions with his team, resulting in increased collaboration and morale.

Why Emotional Intelligence Matters

Emotional intelligence is a valuable talent in both personal and professional settings. It allows us to build relationships, perform better at work, and fulfill our personal and professional goals. High emotional intelligence promotes good mental health, effective communication, and perseverance in the face of adversity.

Carlos' heightened emotional intelligence impacted the entire team. He was able to empathize with his colleagues and build stronger ties as he became more aware and in control of his emotions. His increased emotional intelligence elevated him from a results-oriented manager to a leader who encouraged and supported his team members.

How to Develop Emotional Intelligence

Here are some practical tips for increasing emotional intelligence.

1. Practice self-reflection: Self-awareness begins with thought. Take time each day to explore your emotions, especially in tough situations. "How am I feeling?" Why do I feel this way? How did my emotions influence my behavior?

   - Carlos's reflection: Following each conversation, Carlos began to consider his emotional reactions. He kept a notebook in which he noted times of annoyance or rage and reflected on how he could have handled them more effectively.

2. Improve Emotional Regulation: Self-management requires controlling one's emotions. If you're feeling anxious or upset, try deep breathing, pausing, or walking away to regain control.

- Carlos' Emotional Regulation: In heated meetings, Carlos began counting to 10 before reacting, giving himself time to calm down and reflect on his comments more thoroughly.

3. Develop Empathy: To become socially conscious, you must first place yourself in the shoes of others. When interacting with others, try to understand their feelings and perspectives before sharing your own opinions or judgments.

   - Carlos' Empathy: Carlos started asking open-ended questions at meetings, allowing his coworkers to express their thoughts and feelings. This adjustment in perspective helped him better understand their issues and build trust.

4. Improve Communication Skills: Effective relationship management necessitates clear and open communication. Active listening entails focusing solely on what the other person is saying rather than planning how to respond. Be receptive to feedback and ready to engage in hard talks when necessary.

   -- Carlos Improved Communication: Carlos worked hard on improving his listening abilities. Rather than rejecting his team's worries, he recognized their viewpoints and collaborated with them to find answers.

5. Develop Resilience: To develop emotional intelligence, you must first cultivate emotional resilience, which is the

ability to recover from setbacks. Practice self-compassion and look at failures as opportunities for progress.

--Carlos' Resilience: When things didn't go as planned, he learned to view setbacks as learning opportunities rather than failures. This shift in perspective enabled him to confront difficult situations with renewed optimism.

Long-Term Advantages of Emotional Intelligence

Developing emotional intelligence is an ongoing process that can be enhanced over time. Carlos found that increasing emotional intelligence has far-reaching consequences. It improved both his leadership skills and interpersonal relationships. He became more mindful of his family, softer with his friends, and patient with himself.

The beauty of emotional intelligence is that it is a skill that anyone can learn, regardless of personality or background. Whether you're negotiating corporate contracts, dealing with personal relationships, or managing your own emotions, emotional intelligence provides you with the tools you need to deal with life's ups and downs gracefully.

18

Building Resilience in Adversity

"Resilience isn't about avoiding the storm; it's about learning how to dance in the rain and come out stronger on the other side."

Relatable Story

Consider a woman named Sarah. She was a successful marketing manager known for her innovative thinking and leadership. Life seemed perfect. She had a secure job, a lovely family, and great friends. However, after a few months, everything changed. Sarah lost her work due to corporate downsizing, and her father was diagnosed with a terminal illness. Sarah felt completely overwhelmed as if the world was collapsing around her. The lack of career security, along with the emotional toll of her father's illness, left her feeling cold and exhausted.

Amid her misery, Sarah recognized she had two options: succumb to despair or find a way to survive. It wasn't easy, but she chose to accept her grief and become resilient. Sarah found the strength to continue her journey via therapy, meditation, and the support of loved ones. Her path taught her that resilience is not about being immune to adversity, but about confronting obstacles and finding ways to grow in the face of them.

What is Resilience?

Resilience is the ability to quickly recover from setbacks and adapt to adversity. It is not about avoiding misfortune, but rather about learning to cope, persevere, and emerge stronger. Life is unpredictable, and problems will eventually arise—whether it's the death of a loved one, a financial setback, or a health issue. Resilience allows us to confront these issues without losing hope or giving up.

Sarah's story indicates that resilience is a learned talent rather than an inherent quality. It is formed by small, consistent efforts to adapt to and learn from life's adversities. Exercise increases physical muscles, while repetition strengthens our emotional and mental fortitude.

The Components of Resilience

Resilience is comprised of several key components, each of which adds to our capacity to overcome adversity:

1. Emotional Regulation: The ability to manage your emotions, especially in stressful or difficult situations. Resilient people can remain calm under pressure and control their emotions to environmental stimuli.

   - Sarah's Emotional Regulation: Sarah was angry, frustrated, and unhappy after losing her job. Instead of pushing those emotions away, she learned to acknowledge them without allowing them to take over. She used mindfulness and journaling to help her healthily process her emotions.

2. Optimism: A positive attitude centered on finding solutions and trusting in a better outcome, particularly in difficult circumstances. This does not suggest ignoring problems, but rather believing that they are transient and treatable.

   - Sarah's Optimism: Despite her setbacks, Sarah chose to believe that better opportunities will occur. She aggressively sought new career options, and after some time, she discovered one that rekindled her interest in marketing.

3. Self-efficacy: The belief that you can influence events and outcomes in your life. Resilient people believe they can affect change, even in the face of adversity.

- Sarah's Self-Efficacy: When her father fell ill, Sarah felt helpless at first. But as she took on the role of caretaker, she realized how much she could do to make his final days more comfortable. In the face of uncertainty, she took charge by focusing on how she could assist.

4. Social Support: Strong relationships with family, friends, and the community can provide comfort and guidance during stressful times. Resilient people don't try to overcome challenges on their own; instead, they seek help when necessary.

- Sarah's Support Network: Sarah's friends and family were extremely helpful in her healing process. They were there to listen, offer advice, and simply be there. Having friends to lean on made Sarah feel less isolated and more capable of dealing with her problems.

5. Adaptability: The ability to modify and adjust your strategy as the situation changes. Life rarely goes as planned, and resilient people are versatile enough to adjust their plans when things don't work out.

- Sarah's Adaptability: After losing her job, Sarah was forced to reconsider her career path. She took advantage of the opportunity to explore freelance work and personal projects, discovering new interests she had never considered.

Why Resilience Matters

Adversity is a natural part of life, thus building resilience is essential. Nobody is immune to misfortune, but resilient people may weather storms and recover quicker. Resilience maintains our mental health, keeps us moving forward, and gives us a sense of purpose even in difficult times.

Sarah's experience highlights the importance of resilience in overcoming hardship. While she couldn't control the challenges life threw at her, she could decide how she dealt with them. Rather than being overwhelmed by her obstacles, she learned to deal with them and grew stronger as a result.

How to Build Resilience

If you are experiencing difficulties or simply wish to become more resilient, here are some actionable steps you may take.

1. Develop Emotional Awareness: Start by paying attention to your emotions. Acknowledge your emotions without passing judgment. By becoming more aware of your emotional responses, you can enhance your capacity to manage them in difficult situations.

Sarah's tip: When she felt overwhelmed, she set aside time each day to reflect on her emotions. She noticed that writing in a notebook helped her organize her thoughts and get insight into her feelings.

2. Practice Self-Care: Resilience requires physical, mental, and emotional energy. Make self-care a top priority by indulging in activities like exercise, proper nutrition, sleep, and relaxation techniques like meditation or deep breathing.

- Sarah's Tip: Even when caring for her father, Sarah made it a point to care for herself. She scheduled regular walks through the park to help her relax and clear her mind.

3. Cultivate Optimism: Focus on the positive aspects of your life and believe that better days are ahead. Even in challenging situations, practice gratitude by reflecting on what you are thankful for.

- Sarah's tip: Every day, write down three things for which you are grateful. This simple technique allowed her to focus on what she still had rather than what she had lost.

4. Build a Support Network: Surround yourself with people that inspire and motivate you. A strong network, whether it's friends, family, or a support group, can greatly increase your ability to deal with adversity.

- Sarah's tip: When things got tough, she turned to a therapist for support. Having someone to talk to who wasn't in her inner circle gave her new perspectives and guidance.

5. Focus on Solutions: When faced with a challenge, think about what you can do to improve the situation rather

than dwelling on the problem itself. Divide massive problems into tiny chunks and tackle them one at a time.

   - Sarah's Tip: After losing her job, Sarah made a list of possible next steps, including updating her resume and applying for jobs. Focusing on actionable responses helped her feel more in control of the issue.

6. Accept Change: Life is full of changes, both great and small. Rather than resisting change, strive to accept it as a normal part of life. View setbacks as chances for development and learning.

   - Sarah's Tip: Sarah discovered that accepting her new situation, rather than fighting it, allowed her to move forward more effortlessly. She recognized that, while change is hard, it may also lead to new opportunities.

Long-Term Benefits of Resilience

The beauty of resilience lies in its cumulative nature. The more obstacles you encounter and overcome, the stronger you will become. When you face hardship, you develop emotional and mental strength that will help you overcome future challenges.

Resilience does not mean that you will not face suffering or struggle. However, it does imply that you will be better prepared to deal with life's inevitable ups and downs. Like Sarah, you'll realize that, while disaster is unavoidable, how you handle it is what matters most.

19

Learning to Forgive and Let Go

"Forgiveness isn't about condoning the wrong; it's about freeing yourself from the chains of anger and reclaiming your peace."

Relatable Story

Meet Daniel, a guy whose life seemed to be defined by one act of treachery. Daniel has a long-time friend named Alex. They talked about everything, including their successes, failures, and business ideas. They founded a great startup together, but everything changed when Alex made a pivotal decision. He secretly brokered a contract to exclude Daniel from a critical partnership, leaving him astonished and hurt.

Daniel endured the weight of betrayal for months, replaying the occurrence in his mind and allowing his anger to turn into hatred. He isolated himself from others, unwilling to trust anyone after Alex's betrayal. Every time he pondered pushing forward, the anguish held him back. It wasn't until Daniel had a lengthy conversation with his mentor that he realized that holding onto the pain was just hurting himself. His instructor stated, "Forgiveness isn't about them; it's about freeing yourself."

Daniel eventually began to change his perspective. He learned to forgive Alex, not because Alex's acts were justified, but because Daniel deserved peace. Daniel felt lighter for the first time in a long time after forgiving, releasing him from the heavy burden he had been carrying. Forgiveness was the key to Daniel regaining control of his life and fully healing.

The Power of Forgiveness

Forgiveness is one of the hardest things we can do, especially if we have been severely harmed. It's natural to want to hold onto our hurt and rage because it feels like justice—why should we forgive someone who has wronged us? Forgiveness, however, does not free someone of responsibility or explain their actions. Instead, it's about breaking free from the emotional attachments that limit you.

When we refuse to forgive, we become trapped in the past, repeating our pain over and over. Our hostility continues to permeate other facets of our lives, threatening our mental and physical health. According to studies, carrying grudges can lead to tension, concern, and even health issues such as high blood pressure and weakened immune systems. Forgiveness, on the other hand, can lower stress, improve heart health, and provide a greater sense of inner peace.

Daniel's experience serves as a powerful reminder that forgiveness is a self-gift. It does not suggest that the hurt never occurred; rather, it implies that you have decided not to let it control your life anymore.

What forgiveness is and isn't

Before getting into how to forgive, it's vital to understand what forgiveness is—and isn't.

- Forgiveness is for you, not others. When you forgive, you are not excusing or endorsing the damaging behavior of others. Instead, you've opted to free yourself from the weight of bitterness and pain.

- Daniel's Realization: At first, Daniel thought forgiving Alex meant accepting the betrayal, but it helped him regain control of his emotions. Forgiving was an act of restoring his peace of mind.

- Forgiveness does not mean forgetting. The statement "forgive and forget" is misleading. Forgiving does not require you to forget what happened. Forgiveness is about releasing the emotional force linked with a memory, not removing it from existence.

Daniel didn't forget what Alex had done. Instead, he saw the experience as a learning opportunity. He recognized that holding onto bitterness only hurt him, not Alex.

- Forgiveness is not an indicator of weakness. Forgiveness is frequently associated with weakness, but letting go of pain and resentment takes immense strength. Forgiving someone shows emotional maturity and endurance.

- Daniel's Strength: Forgiving Alex was one of the most difficult tasks Daniel had ever undertaken, but it made him feel stronger. It was not about "letting Alex win," but about regaining his own composure.

Emotional Freedom of Letting Go.

Letting go is a vital part of the forgiveness process. After you've resolved to forgive, the next step is to let go of any residual sentiments related to the hurt. This does not happen overnight; it is a constant process including self-reflection and emotional healing.

Daniel did not wake up the next day feeling completely free of Alex's betrayal despite his decision to forgive him. Instead, he expressed his outrage and grief. He allowed himself to feel those sensations without judgment, understanding that they were genuine. Over time, the intensity of those emotions lessened as he focused on moving forward rather than dwelling on the past.

Letting go does not imply that the hurt never happened; rather, it indicates that the pain no longer defines you. It's about letting go of the emotional baggage that has been holding you back, and making way for new experiences, relationships, and opportunities.

Practical Steps to Forgive and Let Go

If you find it difficult to forgive someone, you are not alone. It's a difficult route, but it's worth it. Here are some practical steps you may take to begin the process of forgiveness and letting go.

1. Accept the Hurt: Before you can forgive, you must acknowledge your grief and hurt. Allow yourself to experience anger, sadness, or disappointment without judgment. These emotions are valid and necessary for recovery.

- Daniel's Step: For Daniel, it was admitting to himself how much Alex's deceit had hurt him. Instead of suppressing his emotions, he allowed himself to fully express them.

2. Consider the Impact: Think about how holding on to the hurt impacts your daily life. Is it making you feel more stressed, nervous, or bitter? Are you missing out on fantastic experiences because you are still focused on the past?

- Daniel's Realization: Daniel realized that his refusal to forgive was making him feel stuck. His inability to trust others was affecting his personal and professional relationships, and he was turning off new opportunities due to his fear.

3. Make a Conscious Decision to Forgive: Forgiveness is an intentional choice. It will not happen by itself; you must decide to forgive and commit to it, even if it takes some time.

- Daniel's Decision: One day, Daniel awakened and realized he did not want to be devoured by fury. He made a conscious decision to forgive Alex, not for his benefit, but for his own.

4. Seek Help if Necessary: Sometimes the pain is too much to handle alone. In these circumstances, seeking assistance from a therapist, counselor, or trusted friend can be quite beneficial. Having someone to talk to may help you achieve clarity and comfort as you work through the forgiveness process.

- Daniel's Support: Daniel sought advice from a mentor, who helped him see forgiveness in a different light. This objective perspective gave him the confidence to take the first step toward letting go.

5. Consider the Future: Once you've decided to forgive, think about the future. How do you see your life in the future? How do you make sure that your history doesn't keep you from having joy and tranquility in the present?

Daniel's future involves forgiveness. Alex assisted Daniel in rediscovering his excitement for his new business ventures. Rather than being burdened by past pain, he focused his energy on creating something new and exciting.

The Peace that Comes with Forgiveness

The act of forgiving and letting go is transformative. It enables you to recapture your emotional and mental energy, which you can then use for other positive aspects of your life. Forgiveness is not about erasing the past; rather, it is about accepting it and moving ahead.

For Daniel, forgiveness did not erase what had happened with Alex, but it did aid in his recovery. The peace that came with letting go was well worth the effort, as it allowed him to fully enjoy the next chapter of his life.

20

Cultivating Mindfulness and Presence

"Mindfulness is the whisper that brings you back to the present, reminding you that peace is found not in the past or the future, but in the now."

Relatable Story

Consider Leah, a 34-year-old working professional who must balance her career, family obligations, and personal objectives. Life felt like a never-ending race, with her mind running to the next task or lingering on something she'd forgotten to do. Whether she was at work or home, her thoughts were constantly wandering, either in the past or worrying about the future. Even in calm moments, Leah fought to quiet her mind.

Leah first learned about mindfulness while attending a stress management course offered by her company. The instructor emphasized the importance of being in the present moment and using your breath as an anchor. Leah was skeptical at first. How can something as simple as focusing on your breathing have such a major difference? However, anxious for a break from her stress, she decided to give it a try.

After a long day, Leah sat in her living room, closed her eyes, and focused on her breathing for several minutes. Her mind drifted at first, fretting about deadlines, making dinner plans, or rehashing a conversation with her supervisor. Every time her mind wandered, she gently returned her focus to her breathing. After a few minutes, she noticed something unexpected: a sense of calm. Her mind began to calm down, and for the first time in a long time, she felt entirely present.

Over the next few weeks, Leah began to incorporate small moments of awareness into her daily routine. Whether she was drinking her morning coffee or walking to her car, she concentrated on the sights, sounds, and sensations around her. She progressively felt more anchored and less overwhelmed by her responsibilities. Mindfulness provided Leah with the gift of the present, allowing her to reclaim control of her mental space and find serenity in the face of stress.

The Importance of Mindfulness

In today's fast-paced world, many of us live on autopilot, with our minds constantly jumping from one notion to the next. We often dwell on the past or worry about the future, leaving little time for the present moment. This constant mental clutter can lead to worry, tension, and even burnout.

Mindfulness is the discipline of focusing one's attention on the present moment without judgment. It is about fully experiencing the present moment rather than being consumed by thoughts of the past or future. Cultivating mindfulness allows you to connect with your life as it unfolds, which reduces stress and improves overall well-being.

The benefits of mindfulness are well-documented. Research shows that practicing mindfulness can:

- Reduce stress and anxiety

- Improve focus and concentration

- Enhance emotional regulation

- Lower blood pressure

- Boost overall mental health

167

Perhaps the most important benefit of mindfulness is the ability to reclaim mental space. We, like Leah, can find peace in the present moment by focusing on our surroundings and quieting our brains.

Why do we battle to be present?

Why do we find it so difficult to be present? The truth is that we live in a world that constantly draws our attention in a thousand different directions. Social media, work, family responsibilities, and never-ending to-do lists keep our minds racing. Our culture encourages multitasking and productivity, which can come at the expense of our mental health.

Our brains are also programmed to avoid discomfort, which is why people tend to seek distractions when confronted with unpleasant feelings or thoughts. Instead of coping with painful feelings, we may use our phones, binge-watch television, or work to distract ourselves. While these distractions offer short relief, they eventually prevent us from concentrating on the present moment.

For Leah, being always occupied was a badge of honor. The more she completed, the more satisfied she was. However, the constant mental clutter made her feel exhausted and distant. It wasn't until she began practicing mindfulness that she noticed how much time she was wasting.

Practicing Mindfulness in Everyday Life

Mindfulness is more than just meditating for 30 minutes a day; it can be integrated into your everyday routine, no matter how hectic your calendar is. Here are some simple ways to incorporate mindfulness and presence into your daily routine:

1. Mindful Breathing: Each day, take a few moments to focus on your breath. Close your eyes and take long, deliberate breaths while concentrating on the sensation of air entering and exiting your body. This easy practice may help you relax your thoughts and return to the present moment.

   - Leah's Moment: Leah learned that practicing mindful breathing in her car before leaving for work helped set a serene tone for the day.

2. Mindful Eating: Instead of rushing through meals, take your time and appreciate every bite. Examine the flavors, textures, and aromas of your food. This not only enhances your meal experience but also immerses you entirely in the present moment.

   - Leah's Realization: After a rough day, she often found herself mindlessly eating in front of the television. By practicing mindful eating, she began to enjoy her meals more and felt more fulfilled afterward.

3. Mindful Walking: Whether you're walking to the car or strolling around the park, take the opportunity to practice mindfulness. Concentrate on the sensation of your feet on the ground, the sound of the wind, or the feel of the air on your skin.

- Leah's Practice: On her lunch break, she started taking short walks outside. She noticed how the fresh air and the rhythm of her movements helped to calm her mind and recharge her energy.

4. Mindful Listening: The next time you're in a conversation, attempt to be fully present with the person you're talking to. Remove all distractions and focus on hearing what they're saying without interrupting or planning your response.

- Leah's Improvement: Leah's relationships improved once she started practicing mindful listening. She learned that being fully present during conversations enabled her to connect with others on a deeper level.

5. Mindful Reflection: At the end of each day, spend a few minutes thinking about when you were present versus when you were distracted. This thought helps you become more conscious of your habits, allowing you to make more careful judgments in the future.

- Leah's Development: Leah kept a small journal in which she recorded her daily moments of consciousness. This enabled her to track her progress and celebrate small victories.

Overcoming the Challenges of Mindfulness

Mindfulness, like any new practice, is not without challenges. It's easy to grow discouraged when your mind wanders or life gets hectic and you forget to practice at all. Here are some tips to help you stay consistent:

- Be Patient with Yourself: Mindfulness is a discipline that takes time to learn. It is normal for your mind to wander; that is what minds do! The challenge is to gently bring your attention back to the current moment without criticizing yourself for being distracted.

- Start Small: You don't have to commit hours to mindfulness each day. Begin with a few minutes and build from there. Even a little attentive stop can have a tremendous impact.

- Incorporate Mindfulness into Existing Routines: Instead of setting aside time for mindfulness, try adding it into everyday activities like brushing your teeth, cooking, or commuting.

- Maintain Consistency: The more you practice mindfulness, the easier it gets. Try incorporating it into your daily routine, even if only for a few minutes at a time.

The Power of Presence

Leah's experience exemplifies the transformative power of mindfulness. Amid a frenetic, tiring existence, she found peace by learning to be present. Mindfulness allowed her to reconnect with herself and her surroundings, giving her a sense of calm and clarity that she hadn't felt in years.

Cultivating mindfulness and presence does not imply ignoring life's challenges; rather, it means approaching them with more awareness and compassion. When we are present, we can fully engage with the people we care about, our work, and the memories we cherish. We find joy in simple times and courage in the face of adversity.

171

21

The Journey Toward Self-Compassion

"Self-compassion is the gentle reminder that you are worthy of love and kindness, not because of what you've achieved, but because you are human—flawed, imperfect, and beautiful in your own unique way."

Meet Daniel, a 29-year-old man who has consistently been his harshest critic. Daniel had unrealistic expectations for himself from an early age, whether in school, work, or personal relationships. He would beat himself up for days over every error, no matter how minor. He could not shake the feeling that he was never good enough. The harder he pushed himself, the more he felt he was failing.

Daniel went into a loop of self-blame and humiliation after experiencing burnout at work and a string of failed relationships. He wondered why, no matter how hard he tried, he couldn't get rid of the feeling of failure. After a particularly difficult self-criticism session, Daniel's close friend made a bold suggestion: "What if you were kinder to yourself?"

Daniel originally dismissed it, thinking that self-compassion was only an excuse to be lazy. However, he understood he needed to change. Daniel, intrigued and seeking relief, began reading about self-compassion. He discovered that self-compassion did not imply absolving oneself of responsibility or ignoring flaws; rather, it involved treating oneself with the same love and understanding as one would extend to a close friend.

Daniel began making minor changes after being encouraged by this new approach. When he caught himself being unduly judgmental, he would pause and think, "What would I say to a friend in this situation?" Instead of criticizing himself for his weaknesses, he began to gently accept them, reminding himself that everyone makes mistakes from time to time. Daniel's intense internal monologue gradually faded. He recognized that he did not need to be flawless to be deserving of love and kindness, and that self-compassion was essential for healing his inner scars.

What is Self-Compassion?

Self-compassion is the practice of being kind, understanding, and accepting of oneself, especially in the face of failure or difficulty. It requires acknowledging that you are human, with strengths and flaws like everyone else. Instead of condemning yourself for not meeting excessive demands, self-compassion encourages you to embrace your shortcomings with love and care.

Dr. Kristin Neff, a renowned researcher in self-compassion, characterizes it as having three basic components:

1. Self-kindness: Being kind and compassionate with oneself when one fails, rather than harshly scolding and criticizing oneself.

2. Common Humanity: Recognizing that suffering and imperfection are inherent in the human experience, as opposed to feeling isolated and alone when striving.

3. Mindfulness refers to being aware of your thoughts and feelings without concealing or exaggerating them. This allows you to manage your discomfort healthily rather than becoming overwhelmed by it.

The Power of Self-Compassion

Many of us, including Daniel, have been conditioned to believe that being hard on ourselves is the only way to achieve or grow. We believe that if we don't practice critical thinking, we will become complacent or lazy. Research, however, shows that self-compassion is a more effective motivator than self-criticism.

When we harshly criticize ourselves, we stimulate the body's stress response, which releases cortisol and adrenaline. Chronic self-criticism can eventually cause anxiety, depression, and exhaustion. Self-compassion, on the other hand, stimulates the body's soothing mechanism, resulting in the production of oxytocin and other relaxing hormones. This makes us feel safe and cared for, giving us the emotional strength to recover from failures and move forward.

Self-compassion encourages a more realistic view of oneself. When we are compassionate with ourselves, we are better able to accept and learn from our mistakes, rather than being paralyzed by shame or guilt. This growth mindset enables us to improve without the pressure of perfection, resulting in more sustainable success.

Why We Struggle with Self-Compassion

Many of us struggle with self-compassion because we have internalized the belief that kindness equals weakness. From a young age, we are typically taught to prioritize accomplishment over emotional well-being, leading us to believe that self-criticism is the only way to improve. This viewpoint is reinforced by a culture that prioritizes perfection and productivity, often at the expense of mental health.

Daniel, for example, believed that unless he kept pushing himself, he would fall behind. He connected self-compassion with complacency, assuming that if he allowed himself to make mistakes, he would give up trying entirely. But he wasn't aware that his incessant self-criticism was holding him back, trapping him in a cycle of guilt and self-doubt.

Fear is another issue that adds to our incapacity to be kind to ourselves. Being fair to oneself requires vulnerability, which includes confronting our sorrow, inadequacies, and issues. Many of us find being vulnerable too uncomfortable, so we turn to self-criticism to avoid dealing with difficult emotions.

Steps for cultivating self-compassion.

Self-compassion, like any other talent, may be learned and enhanced with practice. Here are some steps you can take to start your journey toward self-compassion.

1. Recognize Your Inner Critic: The first step towards self-compassion is to become aware of your internal dialogue. Recognize when you're being overly critical of yourself. Consider this: "Would I speak to a friend this way?" This realization is the key to developing a more empathetic outlook.

   - Daniel's Realization: When Daniel started paying attention to his thoughts, he realized how often he was condemning himself. This awareness allowed him to take the next step: changing his mental dialogue.

2. Practice Self-Kindness: Rather than berating oneself, respond to mistakes or problems with kindness. Recognize that you're doing your best and treat yourself with the same compassion you'd show someone you care about.

- Daniel's Breakthrough: After a difficult day at work, Daniel found himself thinking, "I'm so stupid for messing that up." But instead of spiraling into self-criticism, he halted and remarked, "It's fine. Everyone makes mistakes. "I'll do better next time." This single change transformed how he felt.

3. Embrace Your Common Humanity: Remember that you are not alone in your challenges. Everyone faces failure, disappointment, and adversity. Recognizing this shared humanity might make you feel more connected and less alone in your pain.

- Daniel's Lesson: One of the most striking realizations for Daniel was that his difficulties were not unusual. When he confided in his friends about his feelings of inadequacy, he was surprised to learn that others had similar experiences. This sense of common humanity helped him feel less lonely.

4. Practice Mindfulness: Mindfulness includes being present with your emotions without passing judgment. When you're struggling, instead of pushing your feelings away or getting lost in them, try to hold them with loving awareness. Recognize your grief, but do not allow it to define you.

- Daniel's Practice: Daniel began using mindfulness practices to help him cope with stress. He would take a few long breaths and convince himself that while his emotions were genuine, they did not have to engulf him.

5. Celebrate Small Victories: Self-compassion does not happen overnight; it is a process. Celebrate the simple steps you take to be kind to yourself. Each act of self-kindness is an accomplishment worth celebrating.

- Daniel's Development: Daniel saw that he was becoming more compassionate towards himself. He still had times of self-doubt, but he recovered more quickly. He saw these minor victories as signs of development.

The Ripple Effect of Self-Compassion

Daniel's quest for self-compassion continued, and he noticed a ripple effect in many parts of his life. He became more patient with his coworkers, understanding with his family, and accepting of others' flaws. Daniel learned that being good to himself made it easier for him to be kind to others.

Self-compassion helps not only you but also your relationships and community. When we are compassionate toward ourselves, we create space for others to do the same. We embody a healthier, more loving way of life that encourages growth, connection, and healing.

22

Finding Purpose and Meaning

"Purpose is not a destination to be reached, but a journey to be lived. It's found in the moments when we align our actions with our values and passions, creating a life that feels meaningful and true to who we are."

Sarah was 35 years old and had reached a point in her life where everything seemed to be going well. She had stable employment, a comfortable home, and a few close friends. But something was lacking. Regardless of how many goals or milestones she achieved, she felt a persistent sensation of emptiness that she couldn't explain. Sarah couldn't help but wonder, "What's the point of all this?" "Is there more to life than just going through the motions?"

This existential quandary worried Sarah, especially as she observed others who appeared to be enthusiastic about their jobs or families. Her job, albeit secure, appeared monotonous. She wanted something more—something that would give her life meaning beyond the daily grind.

Sarah attended a personal development conference one evening, and the speaker stressed the importance of identifying one's actual purpose. The idea appealed to her. For the first time, she realized that the missing piece was not more accomplishments, but rather a stronger connection to what was truly important to her. Over the next few weeks, Sarah embarked on a journey of self-discovery to uncover what gave her life purpose and meaning.

Sarah began to clarify her ideas and passions by journaling, reflecting, and conversing with inspirational people. She learned that helping others was more important to her than her own professional achievement or financial stability. This realization led her to volunteer at a local shelter, where she found fulfillment and joy in serving people in need. Sarah's life gradually became more purposeful, and she realized that true meaning comes from following her inner values rather than obtaining outside ambitions.

The Search for Purpose

Like Sarah, many of us have wrestled with the question of purpose at some point in our lives. Whether we're going through a major life transition, unsatisfied with our work, or simply feeling disconnected from our daily routines, the search for meaning is a universal experience. It is a deeply personal journey that frequently necessitates introspection, self-discovery, and a willingness to study what truly matters to us.

Purpose is not a one-size-fits-all concept. For some, it may be tied to professional or creative objectives. Others may discover it through relationships, religion, or community service. Finding purpose is essential because it gives us a sense of direction and fulfillment. It's the distinction between a life that feels mechanical and one that is deliberate and truly meaningful.

Why Purpose Matters

Purpose is more than just a philosophical concept; it has a big impact on our mental and emotional health. According to a study, people who have a sense of purpose are more likely to experience positive emotions, have better physical health, and report higher levels of life satisfaction. Having a purpose inspires us to get up in the morning, especially in challenging situations. It motivates us to continue moving forward, even when life is difficult or overwhelming.

Finding purpose also allows us to deal with life's unavoidable hardships. When we understand what is most important to us, we can make decisions that align with our values and goals. Purpose serves as a compass, guiding us through uncertainty while keeping us focused on what is truly important.

Barriers to Finding Purpose

While the idea of finding purpose is appealing, many of us struggle with it because of common barriers:

1. External Expectations: Society frequently presses us to define success in terms of external accomplishments, such as climbing the corporate ladder, purchasing a home, or reaching particular milestones by a specific age. These expectations may distort our understanding of what we genuinely value, causing us to seek goals that contradict our inner purpose.

   - Sarah's dilemma: Sarah spent years believing that working hard was the path to happiness because society had taught her this. It wasn't until she paused to consider her values that she understood her true destiny lay elsewhere.

2. Fear of Failure: The fear of failing or making the wrong decision can lead to a vicious cycle of indecision. Many people are scared to pursue their actual passions because they are afraid they may fail.

- Sarah's Fear: Sarah was first apprehensive to leave her stable job and pursue other alternatives. What if she wasn't satisfied with volunteering? What happens if she fails? It took time for her to overcome her fear and recognize that pursuing her passion is a journey, not a destination.

3. Lack of Clarity: Sometimes we don't know where to start. Finding purpose can be tough if we don't know what's most important to us.

- Sarah's Lack of Direction: Sarah first felt adrift. She knew something was missing, but she had no idea where to seek it. It wasn't until she actively pursued her principles and hobbies that the pieces began to come together.

How to Discover Purpose and Meaning.

Finding purpose does not necessitate identifying a single life goal or knowing all of the answers. It is about connecting with what gives you joy, fulfillment, and a feeling of purpose. Here are some steps you can take to start exploring your mission.

1. Reflect on Your Values: Your purpose is inextricably linked to your values, which are the concepts and beliefs that matter most to you. Take some time to reflect on what you value most in life. Is it about creativity? Helping others? Personal growth? Identifying your underlying principles will help you understand what makes your life meaningful.

Sarah's Values: She strongly believed in the importance of assisting others. When she realized this, she understood her life's purpose would be to help others.

2. Discover Your Passions: What activities or topics interest you? What causes you to feel alive and energized? Your interests can reveal critical details about your mission.

- Sarah's Passion: While volunteering, Sarah realized her enthusiasm for working with disadvantaged people. This objective spurred her into a major career change.

3. Think about your strengths: what do you naturally excel at? How can you use your expertise to benefit the world? Sometimes our purpose is linked to our distinct features and abilities.

- Sarah's Strengths: Sarah stated that her most valuable skills were empathy and communication. These characteristics made her ideal for working with those that required assistance.

4. Take Small Steps: You don't have to find your objective all at once. Begin by taking small steps in the direction that is important to you. Whether it's volunteering, taking a class, or trying out a new hobby, each small step might help you discover what makes your life important.

- Sarah's Journey: Sarah's journey to discover purpose did not begin immediately. She began by volunteering a few hours per week, which led to a larger sense of purpose and fulfillment.

5. Embrace Flexibility: Your mission may alter over time, which is okay. Be adaptive and open to changing your direction as you grow and learn.

- Sarah's Flexibility: As Sarah began her path, she realized that purpose did not have a specific aim. What was meaningful to her in her thirties could change in the future, and she was willing to adjust.

Living with Purpose.

The next step after identifying your objective is to live according to it. This includes making difficult decisions that align with your values and passions. Living with purpose does not indicate that life will be easy; rather, it means that even in the face of adversity, you will be directed by a deeper sense of meaning.

Sarah defined life with purpose as leaving an unhappy profession to pursue a more meaningful career in social work. It wasn't easy, and there were moments of doubt, but she discovered that living according to her purpose gave her a sense of peace and fulfillment she hadn't had before.

23

Overcoming High Expectations in Finances, Life, Marriage, and the Workplace

"High expectations can be the invisible chains that hold us back from true happiness. When we learn to let go, we make room for joy, growth, and the freedom to live a beautifully imperfect life."

Relatable Story

John was a consistent high achiever. He succeeded in school, athletics, and later in his job. By his 30s, he had a stable position with a renowned company, a family, and a suburban home. However, with each new triumph, John felt burdened rather than content. He had set lofty goals for himself in every aspect of his life—finances, marriage, and work—and they were starting to suffocate him.

At work, he worked hard to fulfill every goal, even if it meant staying up late and missing weekends. Throughout his marriage, he struggled to be the ideal husband and parent, constantly straining to fulfill a standard that no one else expected of him save himself. Financially, he pushed himself to save more, earn more, and plan for his family's future, but the never-ending race left him exhausted and terrified.

After missing an important family event due to work, John realized he had become trapped in a cycle of perfectionism. He had been chasing unreasonable ideals, certain that if he met them, he would finally be content. However, instead of feeling fulfilled, he felt constantly behind, as if he was never good enough. It was time for a change.

The Burden of High Expectations

John's story is common. Many of us have unreasonable expectations of ourselves in different aspects of our lives, including our jobs, income, relationships, and personal accomplishments. These expectations are frequently

189

influenced by cultural forces, family considerations, or our own desire to succeed and be "perfect."

High goals in life can be a double-edged sword. On the one hand, they can inspire us to accomplish great things and push us to grow. However, when they become unrealistic or unattainable, they can lead to tension, burnout, dissatisfaction, and a persistent sense of inadequacy.

Here's how high expectations usually manifest:

1. Finances: You plan to achieve a certain level of financial security or wealth by a specific age. Perhaps you've set goals like purchasing a home, paying off debt, or saving a certain amount of money. When those goals are not met, people may suffer feelings of failure and anxiety.

2. Life: You believe that your life should follow a set timeline, such as getting married at a certain age, having children, attaining professional milestones, or achieving personal goals. When things do not go as expected, disappointment sets in.

3. Marriage/Relationships: You want your partnership to be ideal, without conflict, and consistently rewarding. You believe you should always be the "ideal" spouse, never ignoring your obligations or emotions.

4. Workplace: At work, you expect to be the top performer, constantly achieving and receiving praise. You feel that you should never make mistakes or demonstrate weakness, therefore you push yourself to work beyond your limits to achieve these standards.

Why High Expectations Are Harmful

While setting goals and striving to improve is vital, having unrealistic expectations may be poisonous. Here's why.

- Stress and Burnout: Constantly attempting to fulfill unreasonable goals will drain your mental and physical energy. This is especially true when the gap between your expectations and reality appears too wide to close.

- Perfectionism: When you have unrealistic expectations, perfectionism can creep in. You may avoid taking risks or attempting new things because you are afraid of failing or not reaching expectations.

- Strained Relationships: High expectations in relationships, whether with a spouse, friends, or coworkers, can lead to conflict. When you or those around you fall short of these expectations, it can result in irritation, resentment, and detachment.

- Feelings of Inadequacy: Constantly falling short of high expectations can leave you feeling like you're never good enough, leading to self-doubt and diminished self-worth.

Breaking Free from Unrealistic Expectations

John's turning point came when he realized that his high expectations were driving him away from the things he valued most—his family, his peace of mind, and his happiness. He knew he needed to reevaluate his priorities and let go of some of the perfectionism that was holding him back.

Here are some steps you can take to overcome high expectations and create a more balanced, fulfilling life:

1. Recognize Your Expectations: Recognizing your own lofty goals is the first step toward exceeding them. Take a moment to reflect on the expectations you've set for yourself in many areas of your life. Are they realistic? Are they motivated by outside factors, or do they align with your values?

   - John's Realization: John recognized that many of his expectations were based on societal norms and the need to appear successful, rather than on what was genuinely important to him.

2. Redefining Success: Success does not have to imply perfection. It is vital to rethink what success means to you in a way that is both sustainable and pleasant. This could include decreasing specific goals, changing deadlines, or prioritizing your well-being over achievement.

   - John's New Definition: For John, success has shifted from climbing the corporate ladder to balancing work and family life.

3. Practice self-compassion. Be kind to yourself. It is fair to not meet all expectations or goals. Practice self-compassion by acknowledging that you are doing your best with the resources and circumstances you have.

   - John's Shift: He learned to forgive himself for his flaws. He realized that it's appropriate to set limits and prioritize self-care.

4. Set reasonable goals and break them down into smaller, more manageable steps. Rather than pushing for perfection, make progress and enjoy tiny victories along the way. This method relieves pressure and makes it easier to proceed.

- John's Work Adjustments: At work, John ceased striving for perfection in all tasks. Instead, he focused on giving his all while also making time for his family and hobbies.

5. Communicate through partnerships: In marriage and partnership, it is critical to communicate your expectations while listening to those of others. This allows you to create realistic, shared goals while lowering the possibility of failure.

- John and His Wife: John and his wife began freely discussing their marital expectations. They agreed to prioritize spending quality time together over having the "perfect" marriage.

6. Seek Help: If your high expectations are deeply established, speaking with a therapist or counselor can help you navigate the emotional implications and learn techniques for letting go of inappropriate goals.

- John's Support: John sought therapy to help him overcome his perfectionist tendencies and develop a more positive attitudes towards achievement.

The Power of Letting Go

Overcoming high expectations does not mean abandoning your dreams or goals. It entails striking a balance between ambition and self-care, aiming for improvement while accepting your current condition. Giving up your need for perfection allows you to live more freely, joyously, and contentedly.

John's journey was not easy, but as he let go of the need to be perfect in all parts of his life, he felt lighter, happier, and more present. His career remained important to him, but it no longer consumed him. His marriage became more comfortable and connected, and he felt better all around.

Conclusion

As we near the end of our journey across the complex landscape of mental health issues, it's vital to consider the key themes we've covered and the insights we've gained. Each chapter of this book addresses a distinct difficulty that many individuals confront, such as loneliness, loss, perfectionism, and unreasonable expectations. We aimed to shed light on the path to rehabilitation and resilience by sharing personal experiences and practical strategies.

Reflecting on Our Journey

Throughout the book, we've seen how characters like John, Sarah, and others deal with mental and emotional challenges. Their stories show that we are not alone in our experiences. Whether it's dealing with the weight of bereavement, overcoming self-doubt, or dealing with the limits of perfectionism, the common thread is that these challenges are very personal yet being universally shared.

The first step in dealing with mental health illnesses is to acknowledge their presence and diversity. By discussing our difficulties and seeking assistance, we may begin to break down the stigma around mental health and foster a more compassionate and understanding society.

Embracing Practical Solutions

The ideas and solutions given in each chapter provide a basis for overcoming these challenges. These approaches, which range from developing resilience and emotional intelligence to defining purpose and managing stress, can be tailored to each individual's unique requirements and circumstances. The goal is to make tangible, however small, efforts to improve our mental and emotional health.

Cultivating a Supportive Community

The importance of community and support has surfaced as a recurring theme in our research. Building a network of understanding and compassion, whether through professional treatment, support groups, or just reaching out to friends and family, can have a significant impact on our path to recovery and growth.

Remember that asking for help shows strength, not weakness. It's a vital part of taking responsibility for our mental health and accepting the aid we need to deal with life's challenges.

Looking Forward

Consider the topics in this book to be tools for your own development as you grow. Consider the stories and ideas that appeal to you, and then apply them in ways that appear appropriate for your specific situation. Accept that mental health is a continuous process of growth, learning, and adaptability.

Life is full of ups and downs, and our mental health may fluctuate while we negotiate these changes. We may provide the groundwork for a more healthy and fulfilling life by prioritizing self-care, being kind to ourselves, and remaining adaptable.

Final Thoughts

To summarize, resolving mental health difficulties requires patience, fortitude, and an openness to seeking help. It's about finding a balance, admitting flaws, and accepting that we're all on the path to recovery and growth. As you continue to explore and address these concerns in your own life, keep in mind that every step you take toward understanding and self-care takes you closer to a happier, more fulfilling life.

Thank you for joining me on this journey. May you discover peace, strength, and purpose on your own journey to mental health.

A Call to Reflect
and Act

As you reach the end of this book, it's time to look inward and evaluate how you can implement the insights gained. Mental health is deeply intertwined with various aspects of life, and reflection, coupled with purposeful action, is key to growth. Use these questions to delve deeply into your mental, emotional, and practical aspects, and take actionable steps towards a more balanced life.

Reflect: 50 Questions to Deepen Your Self-Awareness

Explore these questions to gain insight into your mental health, personal relationships, financial well-being, and life goals. They are designed to provoke thought, challenge assumptions, and inspire meaningful change.

1. What is my biggest fear, and how does it influence my decisions?

  1a. Have I addressed this fear, or is it silently guiding my choices?

2. How do I typically handle stressful situations, and is it effective?

  Are my stress responses healthy or detrimental?

3. What does self-love mean to me, and am I practicing it daily?

  How can I integrate more self-compassion into my routine?

4. What is my relationship with money, and does it impact my mental health?

Am I managing my finances in a way that supports my well-being?

5. How do I define success, and is that definition aligned with my values?

Am I pursuing goals that truly matter to me or just meeting external expectations?

6. What past experiences or heartbreaks am I still holding onto?

How can I begin to heal from these experiences and move forward?

7. How do I feel about my current job or career path?

Is my work fulfilling, or do I need to consider changes to align with my passions?

8. What are my biggest financial challenges, and how can I address them?

Am I setting realistic goals for saving, spending, and investing?

9. How do I handle procrastination, and what strategies can I use to overcome it?

Are there underlying fears or habits contributing to my procrastination?

10. What role does love play in my life, and am I nurturing my relationships?

How can I better express and receive love?

11. What are my goals for personal growth, and how am I working towards them?

Do I have a clear plan and commitment to achieving these goals?

12. How do I manage my time between work, relationships, and personal interests?

Am I balancing these areas effectively, or do I need to re-evaluate my priorities?

13. What expectations do I have of myself and others, and are they realistic?

How do these expectations affect my mental health and relationships?

14. What strategies do I use to manage stress, and are they effective?

How can I incorporate new techniques or practices into my routine?

15. How do I respond to change, and what emotions does it trigger?

Am I embracing change, or am I resisting it out of fear?

16. What role does ambition play in my life, and how does it affect my well-being?

Am I pursuing my ambitions in a way that supports a healthy balance?

17. What are my current spending habits, and do they align with my financial goals?

Am I spending in a way that reflects my values and supports my mental health?

18. How do I deal with feelings of inadequacy or imposter syndrome?

What steps can I take to build confidence and self-acceptance?

19. What are my relationship goals, and how am I working towards them?

Am I actively cultivating meaningful connections and communication?

20. How do I handle procrastination in both personal and professional areas?

What practical steps can I take to overcome this habit?

21. What lessons have I learned from past failures or mistakes?

How can I apply these lessons to current and future challenges?

22. How do I experience and express happiness in my life?

Am I focusing on what truly brings me joy, or am I chasing temporary pleasures?

23. What are my long-term career aspirations, and am I taking steps to achieve them?

Do I have a clear path, or do I need to reassess my career strategy?

24. How do I address conflicts in my relationships, and what can I improve?

Am I communicating effectively and resolving conflicts constructively?

25. What role does procrastination play in my life, and how does it impact my mental health?

Are there specific triggers or patterns I need to address?

26. How do I view my role in my family or marriage, and am I fulfilling my responsibilities?

What can I do to enhance my role and contribute positively to my relationships?

27. What are my current goals for personal development, and how am I tracking progress?

Do I have actionable steps and milestones to measure my growth?

28. How do I manage my emotions during times of financial stress or uncertainty?

What coping mechanisms can I develop to handle these situations better?

29. What does meaningful investment mean to me, both financially and emotionally?

Am I investing in areas that align with my values and long-term well-being?

30. How do I practice gratitude, and how does it affect my perspective on life?

*Can I incorporate more gratitude into my daily routine?

31. What are my expectations for my marriage or partnership, and are they realistic?

How can I communicate these expectations and work towards a fulfilling relationship?

32. How do I navigate the pressures of societal expectations and personal goals?

Am I staying true to myself, or am I influenced by external pressures?

33. What are my strategies for managing work-related stress and burnout?

Do I have effective methods for maintaining work-life balance?

34. How do I deal with feelings of loneliness, even when surrounded by others?

What steps can I take to build deeper connections and combat isolation?

35. What are my biggest sources of stress, and how can I manage or reduce them?

Am I proactive in addressing stressors or just reacting to them?

36. How do I handle unexpected changes or disruptions in my plans?

What strategies can I use to adapt and remain resilient?

37. What role does self-discipline play in achieving my goals, and how can I strengthen it?

Am I setting clear boundaries and maintaining focus on my objectives?

38. How do I manage feelings of envy or comparison with others?

What can I do to cultivate contentment and appreciation for my journey?

39. What are my self-care rituals, and how do they support my mental health?

Am I prioritizing self-care, or do I need to develop new practices?

40. How do I address feelings of inadequacy in my career or personal life?

What steps can I take to build confidence and overcome self-doubt?

41. How do I handle disappointment or setbacks in pursuing my goals?

Am I using these experiences as opportunities for growth, or letting them derail me?

42. What does a fulfilling love life look like to me, and am I working towards it?

How can I enhance my romantic relationships to align with my vision?

43. How do I maintain motivation and drive when facing long-term challenges?

What strategies can I use to stay focused and energized?

44. How do I deal with feelings of regret or missed opportunities?

Can I find ways to make peace with the past and focus on the present and future?

45. What does it mean to live a meaningful life, and how can I pursue that?

Am I actively seeking and creating meaning in my daily actions and decisions?

46. How do I balance my ambitions with my personal needs and well-being?

Am I setting realistic goals that consider my mental and emotional health?

47. What are my current stressors, and how can I develop effective coping mechanisms?

Do I have strategies in place, or do I need to explore new approaches?

48. How do I approach goal-setting, and are my goals aligned with my values?

Am I setting goals that are meaningful and achievable, or are they influenced by external expectations?

49. How do I handle procrastination in achieving long-term objectives?

What practical steps can I implement to stay on track and overcome delays?

50. How do I foster a positive mindset and outlook on life, even during difficult times?

What practices can I adopt to maintain optimism and resilience?

Act: Steps to Move Forward

Once you've reflected on these questions, take actionable steps to implement changes in your life. Consider these practical actions as you work towards enhancing your mental health and overall well-being:

1. Establish a Daily Reflection Practice

Dedicate time each day to reflect on the questions and insights gained. Journaling can be a helpful tool for this process.

2. Set Clear, Achievable Goals

Create a plan with specific, measurable goals related to the areas you identified as needing improvement. Break them into actionable steps.

3. Develop Healthy Habits

Incorporate habits that support your mental health, such as regular exercise, healthy eating, and sufficient sleep.

4. Seek Professional Guidance

If you're struggling with any aspects of your mental health, consider seeking support from a therapist or counselor.

5. Build and Nurture Relationships

Focus on strengthening connections with supportive friends and family. Invest in relationships that bring positivity to your life.

6. Practice Self-Compassion

Be gentle with yourself as you work towards change. Acknowledge your efforts and progress, even if the journey is challenging.

7. Review and Adjust

Regularly review your goals and progress. Adjust your strategies as needed to stay aligned with your values and aspirations.

Final Thought:

Embracing these reflections and actions will guide you toward a healthier, more fulfilling life. Each step you take towards understanding yourself better and addressing your mental health needs brings you closer to a more balanced and joyful existence.

THE END

www.ingramcontent.com/pod-product-compliance
Lightning Source LLC
Chambersburg PA
CBHW061038250726

48653CB00001B/150